Joe:

You me the idea of this one!

Keep walking —

Best always,

Martha
July 2018

My Everest

Thirty Years of Hiking
(With Dogs)
Martha Kennedy

Copyright © 2017 Martha Kennedy

All rights reserved.

ISBN 9781975994334

Cover photo, looking southeast from the top of Fortuna Mountain, down the trail to South Fortuna, Kwapaay, Pyles Peak, Cowles Mountain and Mt. San Miguel in the far distance, by the author.

Photo of the author by Lois Maxwell
Interior art work and photos by Martha Kennedy

Maps
Mission Trails Regional Park Foundation
Laguna Mountain Volunteer Association

Gratefully Dedicated to the Dogs with Whom I've Shared the Trail

And to all dog lovers

"Man passes through the present with his eyes blindfolded. He is permitted merely to sense and guess at what he is actually experiencing. Only later, when the cloth is untied, can he glance at the past and find out what he has experienced and what meaning it has had."

Milan Kundera, Laughable Loves

Contents

Hope	9
My Everest	13
Above It All: Vision	17
Medicine Wheel and Hawks	21
Raptors	23
Baby Hawks	27
Close Encounters of the Bird Kind	33
Spiritu Sanctu	37
Shadows	47
Tumblin' Tumbleweeds	49
Power Lines and a Climber's Log	55

Looking for God (in Some of the Right Places)

Panentheism?	61
Symphony	65
Onward Christian Soldiers	67
Shooting Stars	71
Bee! Here! NOW!!!!	75

Dogs and Other Animals

Molly and I Go Skiing	85
Molly and I Chase the Sky	89
Ariel, the Deer and *Riddley Walker*	93
Three Guys on the PCT	97
The Santa Ana	101
Morning	105
Spirit Guide	107
If You Have a Dog…	113
Snakes	117
Snake-bit	123
Coyotes	127
Apparent Reality	131
Night is Sound	135
Punchin' Cow	139
Earth's Spine	143
Home Again	147

Maps

Map of Mission Trails Regional Park	151
Map of Laguna Mtn. Recreation Area	152

Hope — the Backstory

"Perhaps the true purpose of life is simply to express ourselves as best we can. Maybe my ability to keep finding new challenges appropriate to my age is part of the happiness, the thing that keeps me young, creative and full of life."

Reinhold Messner, <u>My Life at the Limit</u>

These days I live in the most beautiful place in the world. Yeah, yeah, I know that's a matter of personal taste, but for me, Colorado's San Luis Valley is Heaven. Everywhere I look I see mountains and vast empty spaces all under marvelous skies that I keep trying to represent in paint (and fail). My heart fills just from the "ordinary" views, cattle lying in a fallow pasture on a warmish January day, flocks of geese heading to the higher ground near the railroad tracks to graze, elk tracks in the snow. I love it. Today on my walk with my dogs I was almost literally knocked over by the beauty of the snow-covered Sangre de Cristos and the lenticular clouds above them predicting snow. Last year, an early morning, spring-snow walk in fog and mist, revealed a solitary red fox running lightly across the bottom of a field, like a dream. I cannot believe my tremendous good luck that I get to live here.

Our bodies wear out. Mine wore out early. I had bone-on-bone osteoarthritis in my hip when I was 52 and got hip-resurfacing when I was 55. Now in my mid sixties, with arthritic knees, I can't hike like I could in the 90s or even the early 2000s. Up and down hills is difficult. Still, I've done some hikes that I almost cannot believe I could do. I've learned to regard the physical limitation as a fixed point, like the time of day or the altitude of a hill. I can't run down, so I don't, but the hill is still there, I am on it.

***

My dogs and I go out in all weather, but we like winter best.

Whenever it snowed in San Diego County I headed to the Laguna Mountains — about 35 miles east of the city — to get the maximum benefit from it. While it doesn't snow often in San Diego County, if it DOES snow, it doesn't kid around. One blizzard (yeah, a blizzard) dumped almost 20 inches in an hour.

Many of my dogs over the years were snow dogs. One was Ariel, a Siberian husky/low content wolf hybrid I got at, well, the pound. She lay on the concrete floor, an undeterminable breed, thin, almost without fur, and with huge, tired-looking teats. I suspected she'd been found with puppies or had been used as a breeding bitch. She was labeled as a white German shepherd, but she had one blue eye and one eye that was both blue and brown. She looked like a blue-eyed hairy greyhound. When she filled-in, she emerged as one of those gorgeous dogs that stops people in their tracks -- in her case, people often thought she was a wolf. Ariel, the husky/wolf, was very smart, very wild, way too intense, but a great hiking partner and I loved her very much. She especially loved winter.

"Going to the snow" (a peculiarly Southern California activity) with Ariel was always fun. Usually we hiked the Garnet Peak trail -- ran the Garnet Peak trail -- blasting through drifts, jumping over plants, avoiding the ice. After Ariel died (rattlesnake bites), I rescued The

Models, two purebred Siberian huskies, Jasmine and Lily, from a woman who found herself in dire circumstances and could not keep them. I got to enjoy snow with these two sweet dogs who -- though born to snow -- had never seen it.

Lily's initial reaction to her first snow — a small patch of snow on the trail — was to leap straight up in the air and land on it then to wiggle around as if she wanted to get that wonderful white cold stuff on every part of her body. Jasmine -- older than Lily by five years -- was more subdued. She touched the snow with her front paws then just pushed her nose in as deeply as she could, sighing as if a life time dream had been fulfilled.

After one big snow, Jasmine and I headed to the mountains where we met two women with new snow shoes. I didn't have any equipment for this outing but a pair of good boots and my old X-country ski gaiters -- and my Siberian husky.

The women got on the trail, adjusted their equipment, and said, "Hi" to my dog and me. We stopped for the moment to respond to their request for directions. I sent them on the loop that led around the ridge to the pond then back to the meadow in which we were standing. The sun was out and I thought the snow would melt down that day, a little, anyway, and I wanted them to have enough time to enjoy it. I had NO idea how deep the snow would be on the north side of the ridge, but I was SURE that the Jefferey pine back there would be coated in snow and frost and I looked forward to the way it would fall off on us as we passed.

While I also planned just to do the Sunset Trail Loop we didn't stop there. We made it around the hill, to the north side where the snow was deep. The pond was our turn-around point, but neither of us wanted to stop. Jasmine was reveling in the deep snow, plowing through it, tossing it in the air, making snow angels, catching clumps of snow that fell from the trees. So, we turned left onto the Sunset Trail continuation that went to Big Laguna Lake. On this trail was an ancient pine that had just recently fallen and I wanted to see it.

Once away from the shade, it was clear that the day was ripening. The snow evaporated in small walls of steam from fallen trees and south facing hillsides. Jasmine and I reached the tree and shared water and granola bars. "You want to go back?" I asked my dog. She seemed ready, so we walked back down the rapidly drying trail to the pond where we intersected the snowshoeing women. We'd covered about seven miles.

"I can't believe we're just running into you!" said one woman. "Have you been running?"

"Yeah. There's so much to see and the snow is going fast up there where the sun is hitting it."

"You come here a lot?"

"Almost every day."

"With your friend here?"

"If she wants to come." Jasmine was a sweet kind of flirty husky, so she was licking the woman's hand. "Have fun," I said then, thinking they'd better keep going or the snow would be gone.

***

The snow never lasted long enough in the mountains of San Diego County, but here, in Heaven, it does. Lily got to come to Colorado with me and, before she died at age 17, she got to enjoy a real, Colorado snow. She, blind and deaf, walked back and forth, and rolled in the snow and would not come inside until I went out and brought her in before she collapsed of exhaustion (and joy).

My Everest

"Hail mine own hill — ye brightening hill-tops, hail! ...loosed from the babbling world, my soul leaps up to thee!
"The Walk" Friedrich Schiller

    Cowle's Mountain, at 1259 feet, is the highest mountain within the San Diego city limits. Like many mountains that are record holders (Mt. Everest, for one), it is an attraction. There is even a coterie of climbers who will not go up ANY other mountain in the city even though the others summits in the range have elevations within a couple of hundred feet of the summit of Cowles. There are Pyles Peak, Kwapaay (Kumeyaay Indian for "Chief") and North and South Fortuna. Having made a few ascents of this Southern California urban pinnacle, and having paid attention to the "climbing" culture, I considered writing and filming *Conquest of Cowles*, a parody of *Into Thin Air*, a film about Cowles Mountain's group of elite climbers.

    I cracked myself up imagining the film. Mountaineers in the latest gear, with the most up-to-date safety equipment, would take to the trail with ropes, carabiners, pitons, crampons, packs — and oxygen.

The Author with Reinhold Messner
(Photo by Lois Maxwell)

How they would struggle! Halfway up, one of them would suffer symptoms of oxygen deprivation, become disoriented and enraged. His partner would hand him an oxygen bottle and say, "Dude, if you're sucking the O's here, what's going to happen near the summit?"

The expedition leader would warn them repeatedly of the time of day and the dangers of bad weather and night, but they would all have summit fever and leave the leader behind in their final push. The O sucker would need to be helped to the summit after littering the trail with oxygen bottles (some would be retrieved by Labrador and Golden Retrievers there with their families). The expedition leader would take his photo, exclaiming, "There! You did it! A great achievement for a mailman from El Cajon!"

Meanwhile, as the expedition members were enduring the hardships of this climb, kids and dogs and moms and dads and grandmothers and fit middle-aged women in flashy lycra would run up and down the trail, sometimes beside the climbers, more often going around them.

Why did I have this idea? Because the "climbers" of Cowles Mountain were, to me, a Colorado "girl," an absurdly serious lot of hikers mistaking that red-dirt covered hump of gneiss for a mountain and confusing a short, hard hike with a legitimate summit attempt. My several jaunts up Cowles were done mostly out of necessity. I worked for the wilderness park that emerged a few years into my Southern California hiking career, and I shot video. I did climb that hill a couple of times for fun.

And it was fun, but, for me, not as much fun as the more "remote" hills to the North where very often, in the middle of this huge city, it was just my dogs and me.

My Mt. Everest comprised the four humps that build the spine of what is known now as Mission Trails Regional Park. It's a chaparral wilderness smack dab in the middle of San Diego and Burbs, surrounded by San Diego, La Mesa, Santee, Tierrasanta, Clairemont Mesa. It's a blessed anachronism, and it saved my life.

I didn't need to "suck Os." My toes weren't likely to freeze off, no chance of a frost-bit nose and reconstructive surgery, no pulmonary edema. *Outside Magazine* and *National Geographic* could not have cared less about the wilderness challenges faced by a little middle-aged lady in San Diego. But if you think about it, climbing at least 1100 feet almost every day for a year? Well, that adds up to 10 Mt. Everests. Doing that — or more — for the next twenty some years? That's ALL the world's 8,000 meter peaks and then some. Not that it's really comparable in any other way, but as I was not in the position financially to head out to the Himalaya, I had to do what I could with what I had.

***

Today hikers post pictures of their dusty boots on social media and review trails on Yelp!, but during most of the years I was climbing my Himalayas, there were no cell phones, let alone cell phones with cameras, no way to electronically and instantly "share" the experience.

Hiking — rambling, wandering — was, unless you had a friend along, solitary. Feet on dirt and rocks, eyes on the trail and, often, in my case, head in the clouds.

Above It All: Vision

"From the summit, all mountains look small" Tu Fu

  If you hike one trail daily through a couple of seasons you get to know that trail very well. You learn the most interesting things about the most unremarkable rocks. You learn how long certain flowers remain in bloom, when the grass begins to dry, bend, and fold; you learn a lot.

  In late November 1988 my husband (at the time) learned of Old Mission Dam on the San Diego River from an article in the *San Diego Union*. The headline was, "Fall Color in San Diego? YES!"

  I missed seasons, and living without them for four years had been disorienting. I didn't know back then which flowers were indigenous to San Diego and which were exotic imports. Life was all bougainvillea, hibiscus and bird of paradise. Not realizing (as the temperatures were in the 80s, flowers were blooming and I was wearing shorts) that Christmas was not even a month away, I had begun shaping our living Christmas tree so it would be ready for the holidays!

That Thanksgiving afternoon I made my first trip to what would become my haven and friend, the chaparral landscape that would become Mission Trails Regional Park.

We parked at the lot by Old Mission Dam and walked the trail described in the newspaper. It runs along the pond/lake made by the dam then crosses a bridge. Beyond that bridge is a whole world of indigenous San Diego County, but we didn't go far or look around much. We just found a place to perch beside the river. Truffle was a still just a pup, only five or six months old, but she seemed to like all the smells and, a springer/lab mix, she loved the water.

The river was lined with golden cottonwood and willows. Some of the leaves, fallen and bruised, sent forth an aroma I had known all my life, giving me an instant sense of "home."

I returned the next day with Truffle. On this visit, we crossed the road from the parking lot and tried an uphill hike. I was not in good shape, and the landscape and plant life were unfamiliar. I learned how much LONGER a hike seems when the features of the environment are completely new.

Truffle and I went back every day the weather allowed, which, in Southern California, was most days. I had not yet learned the joy of hiking in "inclement" weather, or what the chaparral offered the hiker willing to climb a hill in the rain.

Each day my dog and I went a little higher up the trail. In time, I would learn the four seasons of the chaparral and I would learn even more about myself.

***

In March my dog and I saw two rattlesnakes, and we were afraid to hike over the summer. I didn't know much about rattlesnakes then, and ignorant, my dog and I started a summer circuit on the safe, manicured, predictable grass in Balboa Park (boring). When late fall returned, and I felt it would be "safe," we went back to our trail.

In the meantime, Molly, a Malemute/Australian shepherd mix puppy was old enough to hike with us. Molly and Truffle ran free; I walked free. When we all got to the top we sat on a rock, drank water and shared my granola bars. I looked out over San Diego and the ocean. On clear days, I could see San Clemente Island.

One gorgeous, soft, cloudy December day, with everything green, I said to my little wilderness, "Why are you so beautiful?"

At the risk of revealing latent psychosis, I heard it say, "So you would love me."

I protested that I DID love it. It disputed my statement, and replied, "Sure, you love me now, I'm green, beautiful, safe, but what about in the summer when it's hot and the snakes are out? Where do you go then?"

I vowed right then (Truffle and Molly vowed with me) that when the next spring came, I wouldn't run away. I kept my word and hiked up that hill every day through the summer. Because I didn't like rattlesnakes, and had learned that they don't like the heat of the day, I hiked during the early afternoon. I carried water. I wore a hat. The dogs' feet were toughened already from miles and miles on the trail. No one suffered.

I learned that as sere and barren as the chaparral looks from a distance, close up there was ALWAYS something blooming. Summer brings some of its most remarkable flowers, blooms as brief as breath in the stupefying, snake-less, midday heat.

***

I acquired a third dog, Kelly, a year-old red, purebred golden retriever, then a fourth. A beautiful golden stray, Maggie a Girl of the Streets, was a joyful addition to the pack of which I was the leader. She looked to be — and acted — golden retriever mixed with Siberian husky. We had wonderful times, Truffle, Molly, Kelly, Maggie and me.

When fall arrived, I had a sudden urge to hike a different trail. I was physically capable of a longer, more demanding hike. As if testing me further, though, late that fall, on one of the "new" trails (for me) this one up a rough dry waterfall resulting in a "summit attempt" on Fortuna Mountain. (1200 feet), Maggie was bitten by a rattlesnake without my knowing. About a week after the hike in which she was hurt, she began having seizures and died in my kitchen, her head in my lap. I was tempted NOT to return, NOT to risk it, but I knew that the love I'd promised included not turning away when something "bad" happened. There was no malice in the snake; my dog probably stepped on it or passed too close, scaring it.

When I was ready, I went back.

***

"Running Up that Hill" by Kate Bush was our song. If I started playing it inside the house, the dogs began to dance in circles and leap in joy; they knew we were going to run up that hill. We were going to visit our friend, its red dirt trails, its wild flowers, its searing heat, its sudden floods, its winter light, its fragrant blasts of datura scent, its hawks breaking open the sky with their calls, its radiance of, "I was waiting for you!" When I opened the back of my truck, the dogs hit the wide fire roads in a mad rapturous rush, then returned to walk along with me.

The dogs and I hiked most of the trails in that 5800 acres, covering most of the park on long, cooling, summer evenings. The snakes no longer frightened me more than into vigilance. I enjoyed long conversations with coyotes and screech owls in winter darkness, wandering on what I felt was the hand of god.

My eyes trained from looking for changes on my "one trail," I saw things other people might not have seen. I know of a boulder -- well, a small boulder, OK, a *rock*, about 12 inches high -- that is almost an EXACT miniature of Half Dome. Sure, the "people" climbing it, to remain in scale, couldn't even be as big as ants. I know where there are ravines in which shooting stars and Johnny Jump-Ups bloom in February. I know of hidden, tiny, spring/winter waterfalls that are, again, dwarfen versions of swift rivers and cascades in the Rocky Mountains. I know these places inside my heart; I will always know them, as perfectly as one would wish to know the skin on their lover's back, the inside of their own eyelids. They are me, now.

Medicine Wheel and Hawks

"Let us Teach each other here in this Great Lodge of the People, this Sun Dance, of each of the Ways on this Great Medicine Wheel, our Earth."

Hyemeyohsts Storm, Seven Arrows

On the flat top of South Fortuna Mountain was a Medicine Wheel, a Solstice Circle. I don't know who put it there. Witches, Indians or hippies, I never cared. It was a wonderful surprise to happen upon the first time, and was forever after a destination. The first time I saw it was in 1989, before the landscape became a park.

A year or so before, I'd visited my mom in Billings, Montana and from there went down to Wyoming to see the Medicine Wheel in the Bighorn Mountains. I was in my Native American Phase. I had just read *Seven Arrows* by Hyemeyohsts Storm, and I wanted to find my spirit guide. I was pretty sure it was a red-tail hawk because they seemed interested in everything I did. Later I understood that their interest was NOT in guiding my spirit along the correct path, but in taking advantage of my dogs' ability to chase hopping and scampering creatures out from under the bushes.

I didn't love the hawks — well, actually, they were buzzards, red-tailed and red-shouldered hawks — any less for that. Probably more even though, at the time, I was unaware of the very necessary lesson their actual behavior was teaching me -- a simple one, but so difficult for me, "See what's really in front of you. Take risks only for what nourishes you."

In Hyemeyohsts Storm's book, there is the story of "Jumping Mouse." In the story a mouse is shunned by the other mice because he has the misfortune to be carried in the mouth of a coyote who ends up dropping him instead of eating him. When the mouse (covered in coyote saliva) returns to the mouse house the other mice are suspicious. They believed there must be something very wrong with Jumping Mouse if the coyote didn't want it as food. Jumping Mouse is forced to go out into the big world where, naturally, he finds himself on a quest.

On his quest, he meets many animals and learns more about the world around him than all of the safe-in-the-mouse-house mice put together. Ultimately, he's picked up by a hawk who, naturally, eats him. But, in the story, he becomes Hawk and is able to see the way a hawk sees which, from the point of view of a close-to-the-ground necessarily near-sighted mouse, is like having every dream come true.

I loved the story, and I pondered the metaphors of risk and loss and courage. I had no problems accepting that the lesson of any raptor would be the lesson of sight, and I didn't think seeing was easy. I thought it would require a sacrifice as big as that made by Jumping Mouse.

Godnose I'd worn glasses since I was five, but I felt, inside, on a more profound level, occluded and blind. I knew I was missing some important information in my life and I didn't have any idea what.

I started hiking for hawks, with hawks and following hawks.

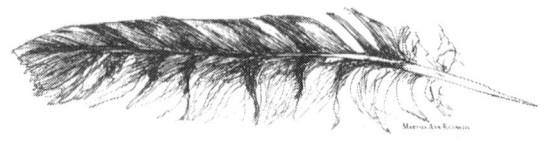

Raptors

"I sure do love a hawk. I love to hear them screech against an empty sky."

A guy I met hiking in 1988.

Most of the raptors I watched soaring on thermals and diving for dinner were not hawks at all. They were "buteos," buzzards.

Buzzards get a bad rap I think because many people confuse the word "buzzard" with the word "vulture." Come to that, vultures get a bad rap. Vulture's are nature's cleaning crew, and we ought to thank them.

Most of them were red-tailed hawks, but there were also red-shouldered hawks which are also buzzards. Over time, I learned the different sounds of the various "buteos" flying overhead -- the red-tailed hawk screeched one high shriek; the red-shouldered hawk would screech over and over again. All this was due to their different hunting strategies.

One day I watched a mated pair of red-tails train their young'n to evade attack from above, and, in watching them, I learned something about teaching. When the little guy did not evade the diving attacks of dad, he got pecked. When he succeeded in evading, mom came up from below and gave him a little lift with her wings.

Because of the dogs, the buteos would often fly along "with" me when I hiked on a ridge, sometimes only a few yards away, at eye level. That was wonderful. A hawk soaring above a mountain or hillside invariably drew me to the top. I wanted their companionship or whatever that was. One late afternoon I had the thrilling experience of sitting on a rock, looking out at the ocean when a red-tail came flying straight at my face, hung on a thermal and made eye contact only a couple of yards away.

I found their nests on poles and cliff-sides. I waited for winter when the mated pairs would return. For watching raptors, winter is the best season in the chaparral.

Along with the buzzards were true hawks like Coopers Hawks and Sharp-Shinned Hawks. I saw fewer of these. Their habits and mine didn't coincide. There were also the beautiful, fleet-flying American kestrels and, sometimes, Peregrine falcons who screeched repetitively. Early one evening as I walked through a sandy wash in the golden moments before the bats living in the oak trees awakened for their hunt, I noticed I was "accompanied" by a big barn owl in silent flight.

The most beautiful raptor — to me — was the Black Shouldered Kite, whose hovering hunt was called by my Italian hiking friend, Francesco, "*Spiritu Sanctu.*" Holy Spirit.

***

The Medicine Wheel (for so I saw it) was arranged with one large stone marking sunrise on the Winter Solstice. In the middle were flat boulders (part of the mountain), and all around them grew a strange and exceedingly fragrant herb whose name I never learned. Molly, Truffle and I -- and then other dogs and I -- would hike to the top. There we drank water, shared an apple and a granola bar. We rested before what was sure to be a fast run down the mountain. I would often lie on my back and watch the sky. Sometimes there would be a hawk soaring so high above he was nothing but a tiny dot in the blue. Sometimes they would twirl and spin down toward me.

Once, hiking to the Medicine Wheel from the west side, up a very steep trail, into which railroad tie steps have now been set, my friend Melanie and I (having evaded a couple of fitness types wearing lycra and plugged into earphones) were met at the top by a female red-tail who seemed to greet us before diving down the slope toward one of the fitness women who screamed in fear.

"She doesn't get it," said Melanie.

"Nope. Not at all," I answered.

"I wish I were her," said Melanie.

Just then the hawk — oops, buzzard — returned and went along beside us for a while then soared north toward a destination only she knew.

***

On another afternoon I reached the Medicine Wheel to find a troop of Boy Scouts moving the rocks. When I asked them what they were doing, the Scout leader said that they had found a witches' circle that "defiled the mountain" because it was against the Bible.

The next time I came up, the stones had been scattered, but the Solstice Stone remained in place. In a strange way, I was grateful for their ignorance though I thought it would have been much more interesting for the troop to camp out there the night of the Solstice and test the stone to see how accurate it was. If I'd been the troop leader, that's what I would have done.

***

By 2002, my first three hiking pals, Truffle, Molly, and Kelly, had all died. None of them young; Kelly the youngest at ten, Molly the oldest at fourteen, Truffle right in between. Molly died in August 2002. Circumstances had led to Molly being cremated, and I had her ashes in a bag. The corpses of the other two had been dealt with more economically. I decided to take Molly's ashes to the what remained of the Medicine Wheel. The Solstice stone remained in position and no one could move the flat rocks that had made the center without moving the mountain.

Truffle and Molly in the Medicine Wheel, the Solstice Stone is above Truffle's Head

The trail was damp and red from recent rains. Clouds split the sunlight over the ocean in the distance, creating patches of light. I was alone, except for my three ghostly companions. As I hiked, I scattered the bits of Molly all along the trail. In my pocket were Truffle's heart-shaped tag and a three-dog Celtic medallion that represented Truffle, Molly, and Kelly.

Once at the top, I lifted the Solstice Stone and dug a hole six inches deep. There I placed Truffle's tag, the medallion, and the remainder of Molly's ashes. I covered them with four small stones -- one for each of the dogs and one for me. I filled the hole with dirt and replaced the Solstice Stone.

I felt in my soul that a long moment of my life was drawing to an end. I lay down in the fragrant herbs and pondered my future, still without the clear-eyed, focused vision of a hawk.

Baby Hawks

*No wonder of it: sheer plod makes plough down sillion
Shine, and blue-bleak embers, ah my dear,
Fall, gall themselves, and gash gold-vermillion"*

Gerard Manley Hopkins, "The Windhover"

Most of the years I was ascending "My Everest," I lived in City Heights, an impoverished, inner-city neighborhood in San Diego. City Heights, during the late 80s and early 90s, was in competition with two other San Diego neighborhoods — Skyline and Barrio Logan — for "highest crime area." My hood often "won." I lived on a quiet cul-de-sac and had great neighbors, but many of my friends and colleagues would not drive there.

I spent a lot of my free time with a group of local teenage boys who lived to ride BMX bikes. Their favorite jumps were at Mission Trails. Very often the boys piled their bikes in the back of my Ford Ranger along with Truffle, Molly, and Kelly. We'd go to "Mission," and I'd drop them off and take a hike with the dogs.

One afternoon after a long hike, I got to the BMX jumps to find the boys all standing around the sumac bush, the patch of shade where they fixed their bikes. All five of them, Jimmy, Jason, Mikey, Craig, and Marc. Mikey, the youngest, twelve years old, handed me a large cardboard box with a T-shirt over it.

"Here, Martha," he said. "These are for you."

I lifted the shirt. Inside the box were two baby red tail hawks, one a dark morph and one light. The sudden daylight scared them and they began screeching and opening and closing their mouths. In their experience, this sudden day could only mean food. I was enraged, "Where did they come from?" If the boys had broken into a nest, they were dead. They'd killed snakes for me, so I could imagine this.

Mikey pointed at a pickup parked near the gate. "Some guy put them under his truck."

"Under his truck? It's a hundred degrees! How did you find them?"

"We were going down to the river to swim and we heard them," said Jason. The boys had done the right thing. I was very proud — moved — by their actions, but it was a mechanically complicated situation. Somehow five boys and I along with two dogs, all the bikes and parts, and now the hawks, needed to be transported safely somewhere. There was no question of leaving anyone behind and coming back later. All the boys would want to be there for everything.

"We gave them some Cheetos," Mikey said as I looked at the little birds.

"Cheetos?" That seemed completely bizarre to me. "Why Cheetos?"

"They look like worms."

***

I love hawks. I want to fly like a hawk. I want that freedom and that vision. I still call all hawks, "My Love." The boys knew this. They pointed to every soaring hawk and say, "Martha! There's your love!"

In those long gone days, if I saw a hawk while I was hiking, I often recited Hopkins' "Windhover," remembering the first time I heard it, recited in a grad school class by John Bayley, Oxford Don, spouse of Iris Murdoch. He stuttered when he talked, but recited Hopkins perfectly. "I caught this morning, morning's minion, kingdom of daylight's dauphin..." Bayley's right hand dived and swooped in the same motion as a hawk flies, marking the swinging rhythm of the poem.

Having since watched hundreds of hawks in flight, I realized that Hopkins had also watched hundreds of hawks and in words, in the rhythm of the poem, he caught their flight exactly.

The boys had heard this very esoteric English major stuff. They knew what it was. Mikey had even pointed at the sky and said, "Martha! Morning's minion!"

***

"What do we do?" asked Mikey.

"We take them to the emergency vet and tell them to call Project Wildlife." I wasn't sure but I sounded sure "But I don't know how we'll get the birds to the vet." The birds were thirsty, probably hungry (even with the Cheetos). They were definitely terrified in the box with nothing to grab onto. They were too young to fly; too young to be comfortable uncovered; too young even to be under an open sky.

If the hawks' parents found them, they couldn't get them back into the nest, and they might not want to. I didn't know that, either.

I was (as were the boys) desperately in love with them. I ached for them, and I was afraid for them. Their chances weren't good no matter what we did. On the ground, they were food for someone, snake, coyote, raven, fox. If I had been alone, I might just have killed them quickly and tried to resist the temptation to put their battered little corpses under the wipers of that guy's truck after smearing hawk blood across his windshield.

I was happy I had to persist in saving them.

I was affecting a straw cowboy hat in those days. A straw hat is nothing but a straw basket turned upside down. Looking at my hat, I saw suddenly how to transport the hawks.

"Mikey, sit beside me and shift. I'll let the hawks perch on my arm and cover them with my hat. That way they can breathe and will be steady on their feet, but won't be scared."

The boys jumped into action. Jason took the dogs and the other boys took the bikes. Jimmy carried the hawks to the truck, his shirt still covering the box. I got in behind the wheel. Jimmy put the box on my lap and I slowly, deliberately reached inside with my right hand. The babies climbed up as if my arm were a branch. I quickly put my hat over them and swung my arm slowly inside the truck. The birds stopped screeching and relaxed, clinging to me.

Wow.

Mikey got in and slid to the middle of the front seat, careful not to hit my arm. Jimmy gently slid in beside him. There was no horseplay, no jokes about farts or tickle-fighting, no sound, not even from the back. I looked in the rear-view mirror and saw three boys' faces looking through the window. We were all pulling for the small lives under my hat.

I put in the clutch and turned the key. We started to move. I was glad we didn't have to turn around. It was three stoplights to the vet.

"OK, Mikey. Second!"

In wonderment, I drove through town with a 12 year old shifting my truck and two baby red tail hawks on my arm.

***

The reaction of the emergency vet was what I expected. Accusations. "What were you thinking?" he said looking mostly at the boys. "These birds should be in their nest! They'll probably die."

I didn't even answer him. I knew how he felt, and I knew none of us had done this. He didn't know how carefully these boys (all of whom were with me in this vet's waiting room) protected these two babies. The vet had eyed us and reached his own conclusion. We were a rough looking gang, I admit it. All of us were dirty; the boys had home-cut Mohawks and some had safety pins in their faces.

Finally, he called Project Wildlife as I'd suggested.

His assistant took the hawks to a cage in the back, and we left.

If the chicks survived, a cage would probably be their world. I didn't know their story, but I knew that no one who hoped to rescue them would leave them in an open box on hot pavement under a truck on a 90-degree day.

***

In so many ways, the boys themselves were hawks.

The boys practiced and practiced and practiced and practiced. I watched Mikey try the same 180 for a solid HOUR until he finally got it right. Getting it wrong meant his face went into chain link, over and over again, bloody lip, bloody chin, bloody knuckles.

I watched them all attempt a can-can over the doubles and fall, and crash, and cut themselves, and break their bikes but they never stopped, they never gave up, they gashed "…gold-vermilion" and got up again and tried again and again and again. And when it worked? It was *"Brute beauty and valour and act, oh, air!"* Absolutely what it was!s

"I really caught air that time, didn't I, Martha?"

Close Encounters of the Bird Kind

"In my room, the world is beyond my understanding, but when I walk, I see that it consists of three or four hills and a cloud."
                                              Wallace Stevens

One of my favorite hikes was virtually straight up the west face of North Fortuna at Mission Trails. I hiked it whenever I could. The problem was that it was not a very dog-friendly hike and the trail was not a real trail, but a tiny animal passageway, twelve inches wide at the most. Only a serious uphill dog would enjoy it. I took a friend up it once and he said, "What are you doing? Trying to prove how tough you are?"

That wasn't it at all. I just enjoyed it. At the top of the hike, were some boulders where it was nice to sit, drink water, say "Good dog!" and eat an apple or a granola bar.

It was a hike I often chose when I was upset about work, upset about money, upset about my brother, upset about one of the universally hopeless love stories of my life. One cold and blustery winter afternoon I headed up that hill with a heart over-filled with something that I no longer remember. It was a perfect day for that slope. By the time I reached the top, which involved a tricky bit of footwork, and I landed on a boulder, I wasn't hurting anymore and had eyes for the world around me.

A "murder of crows" — well, actually, ravens — had taken over the boulders for an afternoon of wind surfing, catching the thermals coming from the ocean, riding them sideways then back down. Several unstrung black kites of joy.

I sat on my boulder about fifteen feet away from the birds, gave Molly some water, ate my granola bar and watched. After a while I realized they were watching me watch them. They began doing increasingly flamboyant tricks on the up-rushing gusts.

They were playing FOR me and competing with each other in a friendly way. Ravens are very, very smart birds with a documented sense of justice and a sense of humor. I watched them for as long as I could without worrying about getting back down the mountain and to the car before it began to rain. That was in the forecast, as I'm sure the ravens also knew.

Once again nature had taught me that there's not much wrong with me that a hard hike and a wild animal couldn't fix.

***

Another time on the same trail I had a very unexpected encounter with a different bird, a bird who would rather run than fly, a bird I'd never seen there — or anywhere — before.

This trail varies in its pitch. It's a dirt trail through scrub oak and sumac, white sage and the wildflowers found on the dry-side-of-the-hill. The slope is between 60 and 70 degrees most of the way; it's a trail that's literally in your face, but a scramble, not a climb. About thirty feet from the top that sunny day, I found I was not alone, never mind Molly who was behind me. This was something else.

It was a road-runner.

I kept going, and he kept going, staying within two feet of my face — at the point I met him was the steepest of the hike. He would hop, jump, step forward as I stepped forward. He stayed in front of me, often turning to look at me, until we reached the top, then I went my way and he went his.

I had the chance to really see him, and he surprised me with his beauty. Brown and white tweed feathers, a dash of bright blue from the corner of each eye across his cheeks, and a small strip of carnelian. When he twitched his tail feathers, they shimmered blue and metallic brown in the sunlight. He was a large bird with a beak that resembled an awl.

Other than this surprising period of direct observation, I knew nothing about these birds, so when I got home I did some research and learned that they are shy, seldom seen except when they're hunting near a road, and they prey on rattlesnakes. It struck me that if they're seldom seen except on roads that's partly because we humans travel mostly ON roads. Still, his camouflage was so good that if he had not been on the trail directly in front of me, I wouldn't have seen him. His feathers were exactly the shimmering brown blue of mottled chaparral shade.

Whatever emotional crisis sent me up that hill that day — and it could have been a phone call from my brother in rehab asking for money, a disappointing letter from a lover, another frustration at work — I no longer remember. But I recall clearly the steep trail, the cool breeze of late afternoon on my sweaty back, the smell of the dust in my nose, and the double good-luck of spending twenty minutes hiking two feet away from a shy bird who preys on rattlesnakes.

Spiritu Sanctu

"Love consists in this, that two solitudes protect and touch and greet each other."
Rainer Maria Rilke, <u>Letters to a Young Poet</u>

"Do you know what we call that in Italian?" asked Francesco.

The field in which we were standing, one of the few places in San Diego County that was still native grasses, native plants, never cultivated, had burned the year before. Burning was part of its life cycle, and I'd been able to watch the blackened earth send up bright pink owl clover followed by bright orange poppies.

Francesco was my student at the international school where I taught English as a Second Language. He was in my advanced level reading and literature class. He was not a kid, but still ten years younger than I was. The first day of class he had asked me if I knew where to hike in the area and where to find the places where the native people had lived.

I wondered how he had known to ask me that. Later I learned that his sister and a colleague of mine were friends.

I was not very trusting at that point, 1994, and with good reason. The turmoil of the year had shaken every bit of my life. I was beginning to regain my balance after a major depressive crisis. I knew I would be making some major changes, but for the moment I was trying, simply, to find some solid ground and figure out what to do next. I was flat ass broke and selling everything I could to make my bills.

Over the summer and fall, my depression had lifted, relieved by Prozac and a clearer understanding of how to control my life, a greater sense of who I was, an improved ability to stand up for myself, but there were now new and even more sinister challenges. Anyone who's experienced a mental breakdown learns who their friends are. I had to go to school every day and face people who thought I was insane. My teaching hours had been cut, and it was becoming increasingly difficult to make ends meet. Because I had "cracked up," the preceding eleven years and all my accomplishments and contributions didn't matter.

But I was still standing. And, in all that, hiking with my dogs was the one and only thing that worked.

I felt kinship with the field, burned out and flattened, I hoped something beautiful would rise up from the charred ground of my soul, my own bright pink owl clover and orange poppies.

***

Francesco had been an Olympic gymnast. He was a mountaineer, a dentist, a high altitude doctor from the Italian Dolomites. He was studying English with the thought of going on for an advanced degree in the US. But in America, Francesco fell in love, and the love was not returned. Heart-broken and ashamed, he gave up on his dream and went back to Italy at the end of his English classes. I say this now because this was not our story other than all the time we talked, hiked, drank coffee together, shared pizzas and, finally, traveled, he was carrying this in his heart. We were two heart-sore people who both turned to hard physical action in nature to feel better. We were friends.

***

On that day, the late November sky was wind-washed blue. We stood in the pale pasture, looking up at a hovering black-shouldered kite.

"Spiritu sanctu," said Francesco.

Holy spirit.

My dog, Molly, was with us. There were no other people that afternoon. It was too late. Most people do not hike in the dark.

But we did.

***

The range of hills was between us and the setting sun when we left the field and headed up the fire road to the top of Fortuna Mountain. Francesco was amazed by the isolation in this "park" surrounded by a city. He was surprised by the wildness of the place. We stood on the boulder that marks the summit and saw the aching gold-brown shreds of the end of sunset in one direction and a full moon rising in the other.

"Wow. Who would think this would be in the middle of San Diego?"

"Yeah."

"And the natives lived here?"

"We'll go back down through a canyon where you can see, but it might be dark."

I was a little concerned about the ankle-twisting rocks on our homeward trail, but the moon would be higher. I never used a flashlight. I'd found early in my life that while their spotty spasm of light might brighten the trail in front of me, they do not light the way. The way is larger than that.

***

Down from the mountain, we turned into the canyon. It was too dark for Francesco to see any of the grinding holes or cisterns left by the Kumeyaay, but we could return. We heard yips not far away and saw in the moonlight a frightened doe perched on the steep side of the canyon behind some sycamore saplings.

Molly took off. It wasn't the first or only time she went to hunt with the wild dogs or chased a deer on her own. Half Malamute, she wasn't so far from the coyotes herself. Truth be told, I loved Molly more than any other living thing in my world at that time. I had good reason, too. I yelled, a frantic, panicked yell. "Molly!!!"

"She'll come back."

"What if she doesn't?"

"She will." Francesco, at home in Italy, had a Malamute of his own who hiked with him and his father in the Dolomites surrounding their home town of Pinzolo, Lone Pine. He was right. Molly came back with stories she could not share.

We went for pizza at a local joint called "Himalaya."

***

The semester came to an end in December. Francesco and some other students planned a road trip. The afternoon they were leaving Francesco stopped me as I was leaving school. "Come with us. We go to see everything, Zion, Lake Powell, Monument Valley, the Arches. Come with us."

"I can't. I," I worried about the man who'd terrorized me into depression, who still lurked in the peripheries of my life in spite of a restraining order. I had no money — literally no money — and who would watch the dogs? Not that they needed it. Their life had been difficult for the past year, too, and they'd learned a lot about caring for themselves because they'd had to. I could leave their food bin on the covered patio, water dripping into their water bowl, and take off for two nights knowing they would be fine. There had been times when I'd had no choice. Truffle, Molly, Kelly and Lupo were a bonded pack who loved and cared for each other. Dogs aren't stupid or helpless. I'd seen exactly how intelligent and independent big dogs can be over that horrible year, how capable they were of taking care of me, let alone themselves.

"I can't, Francesco. I wish I could, but…"

Francesco grabbed my shoulders and pushed me against the outside wall of the classroom building.

"You must come. I will pay for everything. Don't worry about anything. You must come. We will pick you up at 8." I just stood there knowing I would go.

I went home and packed.

Francesco, Fabio, Luca and a Korean woman, Mi Yong, showed up in a rented 4WD Ford SUV. We headed out, driving most of the night, to a motel somewhere east of Las Vegas. The next morning we drove through Zion, stopping to look only for a few moments here and there, enough to make me want to return. It was my first time in that part of the world and I was so happy to feel cold, to look at a frosted landscape, to see a cluster of deer looking at me from a small stand of fir and aspen, red Zion rocks behind them. We took a lot of pictures. The trip would be a big memory, a once in a lifetime thing, for some of them, and we drove on, reaching Lake Powell, a horrifying flat mass of water, or so I saw it, educated as I had been by John McPhee, Edward Abbey and the Archdruid, David Brower..

And we went on. Our destination that day was Kayenta, a Navajo town on the southern edge of Monument Valley.

The hotel was beautiful. The night was clear, moonless and starlit. We settled into our rooms — it would be the only night of real sleep on this marathon adventure of driving and landscape. Down the hill from the hotel was, of course, pizza, and as two of the five of us were Italian, that's where we went. We tromped down the hill to the pizza joint but, on the walk back to the hotel, Francesco grabbed my arm.

"Wait."

"What?"

Our relationship was physically affectionate, fraternally so, but definitely physical. There had always been hugging and hand-holding. It came naturally between us, maybe because we were both people who related to the world physically, but who had adapted to society by learning, mastering, language. With each other there was a lot of talk, but there was much that words could not say.

Francesco wrapped his arms around me, I wrapped mine around him. I was happy to hold and be held and so we stood together for a long time. His flannel shirt was comforting and warm on my cheek. He'd shared with me every residual trauma of mind that fall after my breakdown, and in that embrace, I was sure he felt my freedom. For the first time in years I was out in the world in a beautiful place, on my own. There are few things more healing than natural beauty and friendship. I was in paradise, a paradise Francesco had made possible. I was grateful for the gift and very happy, free.

At the time I did not know what secrets Francesco held in his heart. I only knew that together we were happy and at peace, holding each other in the darkness, anticipating the wonders we would see tomorrow.

***

The next day we went to Monument Valley where my companions had hired a Navajo guide. The rocks were beyond beauty, and the tour was fun. The afternoon's destination was Arches, and the hope was a sight of Delicate Arch. Francesco was driving. I was looking out the window and saw a golden eagle flying beside us. "Francesco, stop. A golden eagle." Francesco stopped and he and I got out of the car to watch the eagle land on a nearby rock with his prey and begin to eat. A curious raven approached on foot, and Francesco knelt, hoping to lure the corvid closer for a conversation. The others were frustrated; they had places to go and scenic wonders to cross off their bucket lists. Luca honked the horn, shattering everything.

Back on the road, Francesco stopped at the first arch we saw. In minutes, Francesco and I had climbed up the arms and onto the top. The top was wide, eight feet at least, and flat. Francesco did a handstand and the others watched from below, amazed and clock-focused. "We have to go if we're going to see the Delicate Arch!" said one of them, so we scrambled back down and went on, pulling over again in a huge area surrounded by breath-taking arches. We wandered around, taking pictures. I felt a strange energy from Francesco, an energy demanding solitude.

The road to the Delicate Arch was closed, so there would be no pulling over, getting out, taking photos and moving on. The only way to see this magnificent destination was on foot from above. "It's kind of late in the day for that," said the Ranger.

Francesco and I decided we wanted to try. We also wanted out of the car and out into the world of beauty that had been calling to us, asking to be seen in the particular way one sees on foot.

"You'll never make it," said one of our companions.

"We might," I said.

We parked, and Francesco and I hit the trail that went first through some black-brush and sage scrub and then onto the slick rock. The sun was dropping; we had maybe thirty minutes of daylight. We began a joyful run on the trackless stone to an overlook from which we could see the Delicate Arch below us. A man returning from the overlook reached out for Francesco, stopping us. "You'll need a flashlight. It's a dangerous trail. You won't make it in time to see anything and without a flashlight you won't get back."

I thought Francesco was going to hit him. What did we need a flashlight for? What was night? What were the risks? I do not think either of us considered falling off a rock or being eaten by a cougar as danger. Francesco had hiked trails of extreme exposure and climbed pinnacles and spires in the Dolomites. As for me? I'd tried to kill myself and hadn't. Neither of us feared much. I think, for us, the greater danger was NOT GOING.

"We're fine," said Francesco to the man, shaking off the man's hand. "Don't worry about us." And we were off.

"I'm a mountaineer," said Francesco to me, exasperated, "what does that man know about me? About you?"

We ran ahead on the gold and pink slick rock and reached the overlook. There in the distance, faint as dreams, was the Delicate Arch, pale rose stone against a fading blue December sky.

"Marvelous." Francesco took my hand. "Marta! *Guarda!*"

But we did have to get back, and that journey was in the dark. Our attention turned to this trackless trail we had only traversed once. It was not my trails of home, the lines of God's hands on which I had walked hundreds of times. Still, it was us on that trail, Francesco in his approach shoes and me in my well-loved, oft-resoled, Merrell hiking boots. From time to time we touched hands and felt the other near. It was so silent and so dark, and in that kind of darkness our eyes begin to see. I had a good sense how much of our trail was the trackless slick rock, I knew that the trail through the black-brush was wide enough for three to walk side-by-side and at the end was a parking lot.

Afraid for us, our companions had turned on the lights of the car so we could find them. They blinded us from about fifty yards and broke the spell.

"Why are they doing that?" demanded Francesco, testy, blinded and irked still, I think, by the guy who'd stopped us, by people interfering with something they did not understand because they could not, would not, do it.

"They're afraid we won't find our way back."

"Of course we find our way back."

***

In 2014, when I was packing up my California life and preparing for this one in Colorado I had the thought of revisiting all the places that had been important to me in the thirty years I'd lived in California. I did not think — and do not think — I will return. One morning as I drove to school I looked over at the humps of hills that make up Mission Trails Regional Park, hills that had been so much of my life for such a long time. I thought I needed to return just once. Thinking of that, I remembered the trails and some of the hikes, then all of them distilled into one hike, my hike with Francesco, the Spiritu Sanctu, Molly running with the coyotes, the bright moon guiding us. All my hikes fell away in that memory. I wondered why, and then I understood.

That night I wrote to Francesco about our hikes twenty years earlier. They were, for neither of us, the "greatest" hikes in our lives.

He has been up Himalayan peaks, Mt. Kilimanjaro and who knows what else in the meantime and I, in my much smaller way, have had "bigger" experiences, but he knew exactly what I meant. These hikes were their own "Everests."

Dear Francesco: The other day, I was driving down the hill (you know I-8 out of the mountains into San Diego). I looked at the hills of Mission Trails where I hiked so much. I don't have any urge to return there before I move away. I feel that what was there was there. I knew it very well, the place itself better than I know my own hands, possibly, back then, anyway. Looking at the hills, I didn't think of all the years of hiking alone and with friends. I thought of the times I hiked there with you. In my mind, I could see those winter afternoons with complete clarity, like a film.

I saw the back-lit black shouldered kite hovering above the golden grassy field and heard you say, "Spiritu sanctu." I ran up the hill with you and stood on top of the little mountain looking out toward the ocean. I felt the sensation of fear when Molly ran off with the coyotes in the dark.

I wondered why that was the only "movie" of Mission Trails that came into my mind out of probably a thousand experiences and then I remembered hiking with you on the sandstone trail in the late afternoon to see the Delicate Arch and it hit me. I think you are the only person I have ever hiked with who was sharing the experience with me with NO translation. We were doing the same thing, seeing the same things, motivated by a similar force. I think we both felt the same freedom and appropriateness both in our physical action and the places where we were. You were the only person I ever hiked with who was not in the least afraid, who felt safer and more liberated on an unknown trail in the dark.

Francesco's response:

Ciao Martha — I have all these feelings in my heart too; I remember a lot stupid and maybe useless things. The moon in front of us climbing on the top of that Mission Trail hill, the golden eagle we saw in the red country close to Monument Valley, so low in front of the car I were able to count her feathers, the Wilson Arch before Moab where we stopped to climb in that astonishing amphitheater, the path we followed in the night towards Delicate Arch while I was asking you: "Martha which one is correct, I would have liked or I wished……..!!!!! But, as you correctly pointed out, we needed NO translation between us.

For me it was the discovery of freedom beside your reassuring presence; the more unknown the trail the better I felt. I can feel all these details but I cannot remember the biggest things: Why were we alone along the Delicate Arch Trail? Where were we sleeping in Moab? Which Motel? Who was with us? I don't mind……..when I think about that trip I think only about us: me and you in the Wilderness. By that time I didn't want to say to myself the truth; but now, after all these years I can speak frankly: doing the same things, seeing the same Nature, fearing the same emotions, matching our bodies with the landscape in the same way……you know how this is called? I call it love.

I will say here I don't know much about love, and romance between Francesco and me never happened, but if I were to think of "love" as I would form it, it would be those evenings when there was no boundary between the natural world and the two burdened hearts traversing it.

Shadows

"...While you remember that unforgettable valley, the valley no longer remembers you."
Beryl Markham, <u>West with the Night</u>

Ribbons the width of our bodies are strung across the earth as we move, shadows skip along a valley and scale a dry waterfall. The world's oldest rock captures our brief footfalls. A pair of red-tails soars above. It is our moment and time rests beneath our feet.

"I brought Subway!" She opens her pack and yeah, there it is. Two sandwiches. One is my favorite, turkey, bacon, avocado and provolone. In those days Subway only had two kinds of bread and 5 different sandwiches.

"You're amazing!" I tell her and reach for it. She IS amazing. No one in my life had ever paid attention to me, what I like, what I don't like, stuff like that, and then GAVE it to me. "Dude, I didn't bring anything."

"Sure you did. You brought oranges, right? And granola bars?"
"Yeah."
"So, dude, what do you think you'll be like when you're old?"

"You'll still know me. You'll drive out to the desert to visit me in your old pick up. You'll have groceries — don't bother coming out without groceries. You'll honk your horn and yell, 'Gus! Hey, Gus!'"

"Who's Gus?"

"Me. When I'm old I'm going to live in an old trailer in the desert and my name will be Ol' Gus. I'll have some old tires in the front planted with marigolds and some plastic flamingoes."

"Why Gus?"

"I don't know."

Inside that tangled hollow of chaparral, those two young women eat lunch, drink water, give their dogs cookies and laugh FOREVER. Their shadow is there, a whisper.

Tumblin' Tumbleweeds

Cares of the past are behind
Nowhere to go, but I'll find
Just where the trail will wind
Drifting along with the tumblin' tumbleweeds.
Bob Nolan

I'm waiting for my coffee to brew, listening to it perk away on my stove. The coffeemaker was made in Italy. My stereo was made in Japan. My TV in Mexico of components fabricated in the US and Korea. The lenses in my glasses were made in Canada and are encircled by plastic formed and molded in China. I, myself, am made up of parts originally designed in Scandinavia, the British Isles and the Alps and adapted for use here in what we — or they — called "the new world." I'm American.

Long ago I taught at an international language school where my students — like most of the stuff in my life, and like me — came from all over the world.

Many of the students I taught would become leaders in their countries; some already were. My goal, as an informal diplomat, was to help them appreciate the complexity of American life, to understand no stereotypes work once you leave the off ramps of the Interstate Highway System.

I didn't often think of the "higher purpose" of my job. It was just something (fun) I did every day. I met them, taught them the English language (as spoken in the US) and what I could about American culture. But sometimes…

In 1995, one of my students sent me a photograph that made me think hard about who we all are, and WHERE we all are. The photo is of me and my students, sitting in the blazing sunlight, on the rocks in upper Oak Canyon at Mission Trails Regional Park in San Diego. It was sent to me by a student from Venezuela. On the back he has written, "I will never forget this beautiful place. And, notice, Martha. Nearly every continent of the world is represented in this photograph!"

I thought, as I looked at the photograph, that if we could just get the whole world on a hike we'd, as my Aunt Jo liked to say, we'd "have 'er licked."

Late that spring, to celebrate the last day of the semester, and the conclusion of a very successful class, I took the students of my American Culture Seminar for a hike up Oak Canyon to the place I called the "Indian kitchen" because of the number of grinding holes, cisterns, and the brilliantly engineered dam that held water in that seasonal stream all year. One of the topics in our class was American Indians and, naturally, one of the tribes I talked most about was the Kumeyaay, the local tribe who had lived twixt ocean and mountains for hundreds of years. I talked about myself, too, about my family's roots in Montana, and of how there really still are cowboys and Indians on this continent, and, these days, a lot of cowboys ARE Indians.

I wanted them to understand the complexity of that question. Overall, my students didn't really understand that European immigrants, still European in language, mind and culture, had settled the continent, killing and dispersing the tribes. Not that NO "Americans" had done this, but "American" was a relatively new creature, and one without any clear identity, either. As most of them came from lands that had been inhabited by their families and their people since time immemorial it was a difficult point for them to get — except for the students from South America and African nations.

I taught them cowboy songs. I like them, anyway, and they are part of American culture. The students loved the songs and sang along when I played the CD making the Japanese student compare class to a Karaoke club in Tokyo. Their favorite song was "Tumblin' Tumbleweeds." (I had to bring one to class to explain the symbol of motion across space as part of the western American sense of self) and they liked a song by Michael Martin Murphy, "Cowboy Logic."

"Cowboy Logic" is a series of "if" statements setting forth a condition, followed by the right "cowboy" response to the condition. For example, "If it's a fence, mend it; if it's a dollar, spend it before it burns a hold down in them jeans." The song goes on to say, "If it hurts, hide it, dust yourself off and get back on again." Definitely the stoic philosophy with which I was raised. All the possible different conditions of life and the ways we could respond to them got to be a joke in our class.

***

That sunny spring day, on our way to Oak Canyon, a couple of tumbleweeds crossed our path. The students were rapturous to see them "live." Their excitement increased the further from the road we walked into this micron of the vast and holy emptiness of the American West. I decided to hang back to allow the group to spontaneously experience the trail rather than to direct their experience. Ignacio — Nacho — an economics student from Argentina stayed back with me and soon the others were out of my sight. Luckily, there was only one trail.

The trail wound through the sycamore and wild lilac, still in bloom. Engaged in a serious discussion with Nacho about his admission to a UC, I didn't hear music. I was surprised when the trail again opened to my view and there was Bassirou, an epidemiologist from Senegal, a lively, magnetic, brilliant man, spinning and leaping in a joyous dance, a wild Pied Piper followed by the International Community, also skipping and singing. Bassirou sang out, "If it's a horse?" and everyone sang back,

"Ride it!"

"If it's a job?" sang Bassirou.

And the answer, "Quit it!"

"If it's a class?"

"Skip it!"

"If it's a trail?"

"Hike it!"

We got to the grinding site. My students first assembled in groups and took pictures of each other, then they scrambled around the rocks. I didn't tell them what to look for; the customs of their cultures directed their eyes and they began to show each other grinding holes, cisterns, rocks, water, plants. Ravens swooped and circled; we ate apples, M&Ms and granola bars, drank water and posed for the photo that inspired this story.

Who were they? Luiz from Venezuela is taking the photo. Nearest the backpack is Bassirou, from Senegal, then Mamadou, from

Niger, both doctors. Next to them, red haired and conspicuous, their teacher. The blond boy is Erik, from Sweden, then Nacho from Argentina, Katsu from Japan in the sunglasses, and in the back, sweet and pretty Onanong from Thailand who wrote, later, "Bye-bye my teacher. Your trip was very enjoyable. I am going to go with my friends again. I have never seen such big nature."

Power Lines and a Climber's Log

You ask me why I live among the green mountains?
I laugh and answer not —my heart is at peace
Like the peach blossoms in the brook, I flow away
'Tis another sky and earth, not the world of man

Li Bai

Fortuna Mountain is not the highest mountain, not even in the little range of hills visible from I-8 East through Mission Valley in San Diego, hills that serve as the spine of Mission Trails Regional Park. I climbed it more times than I can count and, while I know the elevation, it depended on my mood, the air temperature and where I began my climbs whether I called it an "ascent" or a hard walk. Of course, noon on an August day could be a killer, especially on the dogs, so I carried a gallon of water or more. Weighed down like that, it was no picnic for me either — or was it?

The first time I climbed Fortuna was in 1988. Mission Trails Regional Park was barely a park. There was no visitor's center, or marked trails or anything people are used to today. It was October and very hot. I reached the "summit" just before sunset. A cool wind almost always blows up there, and I took off my boots and socks and left everything to dry. I was uninitiated into such things as wool or polypro hiking socks that wick moisture (I wore cotton) and trail running shoes had barely been developed. I was wearing Swiss made *"kletters."* I ate a granola bar and looked around. There was nothing. Miles and miles of nothing. Chaparral and silence. I was so happy.

I began going up that mountain every time I had a couple of hours to spare. In spring I walked through corridors of wild lilac. Lying on the top, I watched swifts fly around me, zooming down to check me out and then darting off to report to the others. Hawks surfed the thermals, rising and falling, hunting. Sometimes a lizard sunned itself on a rock below; once a garter snake pointed downslope, leading my eyes to a big deer looking into the distant.

And it was silent. There was no HWY 52.

Solitude. What defines a human, in my mind, is the ability to sit with the self. I approached that mountain from every angle, sometimes crossing the river from the end of Jackson Drive, hiking up Suycott Wash, then an almost straight up climb along a ridge on the west "face" of Fortuna. Sometimes I hiked up Oak Canyon from Old Mission Dam, following the power lines, a right turn at the saddle of the fire road, then a right turn to the top. Sometimes up the face of South Fortuna (no steps back then) then across the trail from Fortuna to Fortuna.

***

One Sunday, just as I left Oak Canyon and began the climb up the fire road to Fortuna, I ran into a nervous, morning hiker, stressed on the subject of "direction." He asked me, "Where's Fortuna Mountain?"

I said, "It's that big one up there," and I pointed behind him and fished a map out of my pack.

"Where?" he asked.

"Up there." I pointed, helpfully, perhaps.

"How can I get there?"

"Just follow this fire road and at the hump, turn right, keep climbing and you'll be there."

"What about the power lines?" he asked. "Won't I get a brain tumor?"

"You could get a brain tumor," I answered. "I guess that's always possible, power lines or not, but you'll also get to the top of the mountain."

"Naw," he said. "Too dangerous."

I met him again months later. He recognized me. "Hi," he said. "I've been wanting to thank you for the map. I found Fortuna. You were right. It's a great hike."

***

For anyone who attempted the dangers, the rewards were real — scenery, fresh air and a sense of freedom — and a coffee can filled with scraps of paper. Yes, for a while this little hump of a hill had a "Climbers' Log."

The first time I saw it, I was annoyed. "What? Other people on MY mountain? How DARE they?" However, through time the log began to grow, and some of the scraps of paper had become worn, damaged by rain and time; others were new. All of them were interesting; some of them were profound and a few made me laugh. That search for solitude seemed to make people reach out to others, sharing thoughts and welcoming thoughts. Some of the notes formed dialogues. I brought the papers home with me, thinking of buying a metal box and a book to protect them.

"Been looking at this mountain for 37 years. Finally made it up."

"Nature is alive up here! Nice hike! Keep it clean!"

"Just keeping tabs on 'the hood'. Development? Highways? What happened to three valleys and all the DIRT BIKES? Some things never change."

"It's almost like being on Cloud 7!"

"Big rains last night. Lots of water in the creek beds. Not a crystal view, but moist, lush and a little hazy. Thanks for keeping the trash picked up. Route 52 is a drag."

Of all the messages I read, this was my favorite:

"I'm a kid, hikeing (sic) from Cowles' Mt. with my dad. I love this place. In conclusion, this is a 15 mile hike."

***

The most intriguing discovery, as I read all of these messages in a bottle, was in the variety of people climbing "my" mountain. There was no "type," but there was harmony in the experience of viewing the horizon in all directions. There was the physical achievement, the sense of reaching "cloud 7" — the semi-top of the world. But something else seemed to happen.

Down below, we human giants shove through the traffic jams of our human problems and we feel so big, as if everything has to be arranged and controlled and changed by us. We blunder our way through relationships, compete our way through our jobs, meeting deadlines that seem like the end of the world, and we hate ourselves when we "fail." I realized that the mountain added about a thousand feet to the height of everyone who climbed it, but the writers of the messages didn't seem to feel bigger or more powerful.

There, at the highest altitude of all our effort, everyone seemed reminded of their true scale in the universe, as someone wrote, *"Everywhere I look, I see the hand of God."*

Looking for God

(in Some of the Right Places)

Panentheism?

My home is Blue Ridge Peak;
I roam the primeval void.
Who will go with me to keep me company?
Returning to the great waste of infinity.

Cao Xueqin <u>The Story of the Stone</u>

  I'd spent the day hiking in the Lagunas and had gone into town to meet friends for dinner. All the people at the table were devout, fundamentalist Christians. One, Kris, had been my student and had become my main hiking pal. We hiked and talked and hiked and talked and watched hawks and talked about gear and shoes and seeing a mountain lion. Kris' friend, Fred, had been his philosophy and religion teacher. The kids around the table were Fred' nephews.

  I liked all of them very much, and I liked the restaurant. Kris had picked me up, then we stopped for Fred's oldest nephew and headed down the mountain. By then I was living in the Cuyamaca Mountains in the town of Descanso which is Spanish for "I rest."

That day, because I had had a lot of grading to do, I was going out and my time was limited, I hiked fast through fog and mist, a little drizzle, beads of water clinging to pine needles and tall grass, a simple, short, familiar hike for me. The backside of the ridge was a narrow trail, always somewhat mysterious and eerie. I often ran that segment. That day I ran in the mist, savoring the smells and dreading the numerous ticks that my dogs were picking up. I was hiking with The Models, the two Siberian Huskies who came to live with Lupo and me after Ariel died.

The Models: Jasmine (back) and Lily

Kris had dubbed them "The Models" because they were so beautiful. He said that for Lupo, my old male dog, my getting Jasmine and Lily would have been like his parents bringing home a couple of Swedish models for him to live with. Jasmine and Lily learned to come when I yelled, "Models!" Though they had to be leashed, they were peaceful friends on the trail — and trails were new to them when they first came to live with me.

We reached the granite outcropping with its little ledge that looked over a brush filled ravine, the drainage for the pond. The clouds filled the ravine in trembling veils, moving quickly toward the pond which, when we reached it, pulled the veils of mist down to its cooler surface, held them for a moment, then released them to rise higher, to touch the high pines, to vanish. I sat on a rock for a while watching this beautiful phenomenon of temperature.

Still filled with these images, I sat down at the table with my friends. Kris was to my right. Little Liam, only six years old, was to my left. I had not met Liam before, and found him to be an enchanting kid, full of life and questions.

Fred asked about my walk and I told him about the mist, the fog, the drizzle, the beauty of it, the ticks I'd pulled of the models and the pond.

"That sounds beautiful!" said little Liam.

"It was," I said. "Do you want me to draw a picture of it?"

"Yes!" I knew from experiences drawing animals at the zoo how much kids like to watch someone draw.

I turned over my placemat and drew the pond, the hill behind it, trees on the side.

"Where is the mist?"

"I'm getting there." I had the idea of "animating" the mist, drawing from the lower part o the ravine up to the pond and then letting my pen "lift off" the surface. This is what I did.

"I've seen that, " said Fred. "It's quite something."

"Can I keep it?" asked Liam, about the picture.

"Sure." I didn't think I needed a placemat anyway.

Then Liam asked me, "Martha, are you a pantheist or a panENtheist."

"What?" *Good God,* I thought, *you're six.*

"Are you a pantheist or a panentheist?"

"That's a good question," said Fred. Truly the ONLY topic of conversation with this family was God.

"What's the difference? I know what a pantheist is, but what's a pannantheist?" I was trying to joke my way out of this.

"I can tell her. Can I tell her? Let me!" Liam was on it and didn't want Uncle Fred to take over.

"Sure, Liam. If you get stuck, I'll help, OK?"

"OK. OK, Martha, a pantheist believes God is in everything but a panentheist believes everything is God."

My brain hurt, and Liam was six.

"I don't see the difference."

"God is IN everything or everything IS God. See? It's easy, Martha."

"No."

Fred jumped in and gave a professorial explanation that made me grateful when the food came.

"I gotta' think about that," I said. I really needed to read about it. My aural learning ability has been legitimately measured as zero.

I later learned that Liam hung the drawing on his bedroom wall. And as for me? The question was good. There is a huge difference between God being IN everything as an ingredient, and everything, all together, the entire universe, every particle, dog hair, fallen lilac petal, screeching hawk, silent searching owl, angry ground squirrel, frost-cracked rock being God, a giant, divine and ever-changing unit of being, through which I, a particle of God, walked.

Symphony

"All things are in motion, all is in process, nothing abides, nothing will ever change in this eternal moment."
Edward Abbey, *Desert Solitaire*

One winter day I was driving home from hiking. I turned the radio to the classical music station. They were playing the *Eroica*. It was hard to hear because of interference from static, a nearby hip-hop station and traffic noises. I focused on the symphony and refused to be irritated by the extra noise or even to listen to it. What I did hear was a marvelous metaphor.

There was the incomparable melody, magic, pure, passionate and integral. Next to it, twining through it, there was distracting noise.

I thought that is a pretty good summary of my life. There is a melody, pure, passionate and integral, and there is static, side noise, sometimes loud and insistent — always distracting — I've been frequently distracted, and the melody remaining on its course like a beautiful line straight and true that more than belongs to me, IS me.

That day I had seen a roadrunner — the second time in my life. Seeing a roadrunner is always a mysterious encounter as the birds are very shy. I was hiking to the remains of the Medicine Wheel, feeling pangs of loss for Truffle, Molly, and Kelly. I remembered all the times I was up there with Molly, how I would sit on the big center rock mass and hold her, my legs spread out around her, and stroke her nose, and, when she was a pup, I scratched her belly. I thought of Truffle's immense thirst and how I knew she'd rather be "fishing" and Kelly? That mysterious creature simply followed, her joy quiet, subdued, possibly, by her first year of life as an unloved backyard dog.

I was now surrounded by different dogs, Ariel, Mila and Persephone — Ariel was a white Siberian husky/wolf dog, Mila a Chow-chow mix and Persephone was a brindle pit bull. I was living a completely different life.

The constant? These hills, this place, the joy in my existence, teaching, a novel in progress — my first — made up the thread of the melody. Suddenly I thought, "Clogging the mind with what does not belong to you leaves no space for what does."

I wondered how to write a story about it, finally seeing it as a film, with music to the sides and songs leading into the detours, the biological detour of gender, the philosophical detour of Christianity and marriage, the sensual detours of sex, the detours, distractions. Those things which are not detours become the symphony; they are harmonious with the melody, they are motifs, leitmotifs, interludes all that make the song more than a note. The challenge is to hold to the main line of the composition while still living courageously enough to venture outward in discovery of the song. How to know what is what? What is part of the piece, what is a distraction? Maybe all that matters is that when you get lost, you find your way back.

Onward Christian Soldiers

In whose hand is the soul of every living thing, and the breath of mankind?
Job 12:10

    I got up early to make an early start. Still a novice at hiking in the chaparral, I thought I had to get an early start. Why? To avoid the heat of the day? (Ha!) To hit the trail before the thunderstorms gathered? (A problem of the Rocky Mountains; very unlikely in the chaparral.) In time I learned the best time for me to hike was in the late afternoon when the day got cooler as I went along and the light more beautiful.

    But I didn't know that yet.

    I leashed Truffle and Molly and we headed to Mission Trails to climb Big Dog — Kwaay Paay — that Sunday morning in May.

    I parked the car in the lot at Old Mission Dam, crossed the road and found our trail. We bushwhacked. I like to bushwhack if it's not too nasty. I like straight up hills, and I was in a hurry that morning to get to the top. I don't remember why. It was probably just some "Run up the mountain!" internal pressure, the need to get outside and push my body. I wasn't in a good mood, I remember that, and I hoped getting outside with the dogs would help. It usually did.

But not that day.

We followed a coyote trail up the "face" of the "mountain." Halfway up, I saw a group of eight young men on the trail to my left. They were singing "Onward Christian Soldiers."

"OK, that's YOUR business," I thought, "just don't get to the top before I do. I don't want to share it with you."

Truffle, Molly and I began to run. We reached the trail along the ridge, my dogs, as always, running ahead. There, four feet away, between my dogs and me, was a gorgeous, mature, red diamondback rattlesnake warming up, greeting the day. The dogs ran over her several times until, when they finally came to me, I leashed them. Because of the boys, not because of the snake -- she was cold and not interested in any of us. One thing I learned after only a few encounters with rattlesnakes is that they're interested in what they can eat and they can tell the difference between food and not food, especially an old snake like this one. If that were not the case many more people would be bit each year. As it is, a person has to have excruciatingly bad luck, be abysmally stupid or have an unrealistic sense of his mortality to be bitten. It's a sad commentary on humanity that upwards of 300 people are bitten by rattlesnakes every year in California -- with an average of one fatality.

"Damn," I thought. I tried to move her off the trail using my hiking stick, but she was still too cold.

Meanwhile, no longer distant, came "Onward Christian Soldiers."

I decided to go down the trail a bit between her and the "army" so I could warn them.

"There's a big red diamondback in the trail in front of you," I said when they reached me.

"What? No way. I want to see." Before I could say, "Leave it alone," they were past me. Within seconds I could hear them shrieking and then the beating began. They picked up sticks and rocks and pulverized the snake.

I wanted to kill them.

I headed down the mountain, sickened. Probably if I'd said nothing, they would not have noticed her, camouflaged as she was. But they might have stepped on her. I had hoped to avoid that. I was wrong in assuming they would just walk around her. I felt I'd killed her.

One of the boys yelled down at me, "Hey, you can come back up. We killed the snake. It's safe now."

"Fuck you," I thought. "You're the danger."

Over time, I began to see the whole thing as symbolizing human's relationship with earth. I'd say, on the whole, we just don't get it.

And I hate that song.

Shooting Stars

Full many a flower is born to blush unseen,
And waste its sweetness on the desert air.

Thomas Gray, "Elegy Written in a Country Churchyard

Just as those "Onward Christian Soldiers" serpent-slaughtering boys went up the mountain in search of some kind of Christian spiritual experience, I was looking for something. An answer? I didn't know the question. A spiritual awakening? I didn't know, but day after day, in all weather, I was up there on that hill looking. Sometimes my turn-around point was after looking out over the ocean at sunset, other days it was looking back at the distant Cuyamaca Mountains after they'd been hit by a winter storm.

I found new trails I loved and hiked them; a razor edge ledge where, after a winter storm, the clouds billowed up from the ocean and tangled with the higher hills. There I could walk in the clouds. There was a granite outcropping between the ledge and the main trail where I sometimes sat with my dogs and looked out over the valley, the San Diego River, swollen with El Niño rains, the distant hills as yet unknown to me. There was a cleft between two hills where a waterfall ran after rains, and in February, shooting stars bloomed.

The wildflowers were little "bits" of Colorado in my rambling. But they were more than that.

Snatches of poetry often wandered through my mind on my rambles, such as Robert Service' poem, "The Call of the Wild" — "Have you seen God in His splendours, heard the text that nature renders?" I was increasingly open to that book. The best thing in my life was this hill.

The shooting star reached down into the depths of my memory to something I'd learned as a junior in high school, something I didn't like and, at the time, repudiated as not applicable to me. "Elegy Written in a Country Churchyard" by Thomas Gray. You see, I had grand goals.

Then one afternoon I sat on a damp and mossy rock deeply appreciating these tiny lavender flowers with their black and yellow heads, their stems delicate and graceful, arching toward the quiet cool light of Southern California's brief spring, and here came Thomas Gray…"Full many a flower is born to blush unseen, And waste its sweetness on the desert air."

I wasn't going to let this happen to "my" shooting stars. They were NOT going to "blush" unseen. It became my mission every year, wherever I was hiking in the convolution of hills, to seek out the small, shaded clefts of stone and see the shooting stars.

And one year a miracle happened.

I had long abandoned my one hill, and ranged far, far afield in eight, ten, twelve-mile hikes. Still I kept my promise and when February came, and the weather was at the point where these little flowers bloomed, I was there on shady hillsides looking for narrow ravines where I might find them. Over the years, I identified dozens of these small places and had come to understand that "my" chaparral was exactly like a major mountain range — in miniature.

On this day, I had spent hours and hours — too many hours — correcting essays. I barely made it outside in time to have a decent hike. I got to the park and headed up a very steep fire-road to a ridge trail that hung above Suycott wash. On the fire road trail above THAT were vernal pools and chocolate lilies in their season. It was a wide, red trail for bikes and birders, a small detour led to a cul-de-sac where some yoga aficionado had set a wooden meditation stool.

At the exact right spot, I turned up toward the high trail, climbing beside the rift where the flowers were blooming. All I had to do was look at them and, maybe, mentally, thank them for being there and for what I'd learned from looking for and at them over time. I was looking into the mirror of nature and beginning to get it. Maybe it was only because I was old enough, had failed enough. Maybe I was learning to "read the text that nature renders."

On top of the hill, straight up from, on the red fire road, out of my sight, a man in a wheel-chair and his son looked out over the valley. Everything was splendidly green in the chaparral's necessary opportunistic rush to bloom, spawn and seed.

I emerged a few feet from them. They would have seen a too-red mop of hair and then me.

"Hi."

"Hi," said the son.

"Hi," said the dad.

I happened to be with my golden retriever Kelly that day. She was happy to meet everyone, and the man in the wheelchair was happy to pet her. I noticed his hands were spastic and awkward, and once in a while his foot seized up in a spasm. I suspected Multiple Sclerosis.

My dad died of MS when I was 20. I was so young that it was shocking to me that my will-power and love had not saved his life. Our family was shattered by his illness, my mother broken by his death.

We talked. The man's voice was clear with a little evidence of struggle to get words out, but nothing bad, not incomprehensible. He and his son clearly had a great friendship. A woman and a teenage girl approached and the man said, "Honey, this is Martha and this is Kelly." Kelly's tail spun like a helicopter propeller. We all shook hands, even Kelly.

We chatted for a few minutes. It came out that this was the man's birthday, and he had wanted to go on a hike. These were his children; this was his wife. And I had been right; he had MS. We talked a bit longer and then I said I had to keep going or I wouldn't be home in time to feed Kelly.

"It was nice meeting you!" said the woman.

"Hope to see you again," said the man.

"Me too," I said and Kelly and I took off running. My heart was full. Here was a family — just like mine had been — but not broken. The dad and son were friends. The mom and the daughter were friends. Somehow this horrible disease did not seem to have destroyed them. They were enjoying a Sunday hike — dad in a wheelchair. Just like that. Just like it was life.

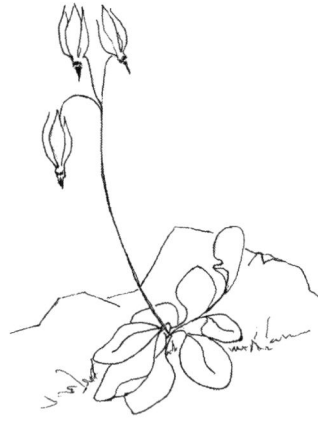

What a gift the shooting stars had given me. One I would not have had if I had allowed them to "…blush unseen, And waste their sweetness on the desert air."

Bee! Here! NOW!!!

"Some colors you never saw again because each ay the light was different, and often the colors you saw yesterday never came back"

Beryl Markham, "The Captain and the Horse"

Soon after I moved to San Diego from Denver I got a job I loved. I was teaching English as a Second Language at an international school attached to a university. My salary was almost TWICE as much (numerically) as I was earning in Denver. I was on cloud 10.

I remember the first day of school very well. I went. I taught my two morning classes, and then I wandered around the campus looking for a spot to have lunch. I ended up on a concrete bench next to a rose garden in front of what San Diego State University would call "Old Main" if it called any of its buildings "Old Main."

I couldn't believe my awesome luck as I ate my peanut butter sandwich and drank my Tab. I felt that way about San Diego State until I moved away. It was a dream come true.

A guy I'd met at the beach had said, "People move to California, and they either get oranges or they go home." I thought I had definitely had gotten oranges.

The reality was that I got a kind of "orange salad." I didn't fit in with my colleagues. After a year, I'd learned about professional competitiveness, and I'd experienced the aggressive rift between the two basic ways of teaching. Each style is absolutely tied to personality. Many teachers approach their classes and the curriculum systematically, methodically. They are linear, detail-oriented people who follow rules. I was relatively new to teaching and only beginning to realize that while I used good methods, I was not this kind of teacher. I thought a lot of about internal and external motivation, and I thought internal motivation — desire — was more likely to lead to success in studying something as mind-numbing as English Grammar or as daunting as writing in a new language. I believed the greatest teaching tool I had was my students' desire to learn. I saw my job as awakening that desire. Then they would WANT to complete the steps necessary to master whatever was being taught in the class. I evolved into an inspiring teacher. That's <u>not</u> bragging. It's not an easy road because it depends too much on personality. Students have problems with it because it challenges them, and colleagues don't appreciate it. For years I was literally "shunned" by my colleagues who labeled me as "creative" which they saw as synonymous with unreliable.

My personal belief is that BOTH kinds of teachers are necessary to create a dynamic learning environment for students. I respected my colleagues whether they "got" me or not. Fortunately, my bosses understood.

So there I was. Teaching and hiking, teaching and hiking, teaching and hiking, trying to write, teaching and hiking, hanging out with the kids in the neighborhood, teaching and hiking. Hiking.

Over time my colleagues began to notice that I was OK with their shunning. Some of them began to wonder if I didn't have a point, maybe I was right about something, and they began including me. By then, however, I was off on my own trajectory, no longer looking for friends among them. A colleague, Christine, had actively and openly disliked me. She told me so. But (to my surprise) after a few years, she began "courting" my attention and trying to be friends. It appeared that her fairy-tale marriage to the handsome guy she'd met while teaching in eastern Europe was falling apart. The little boy they'd had to save their marriage was turning out to be just a little boy who needed his parents in a disintegrating family. My own marriage wasn't going very well, either. Maybe it was the time in our lives. Maybe it was just the way it was. We became friends.

It was the early 1990s and there was, as always, a variety of "spiritual" theories in the ether. Christine was floundering around looking for something to fill an empty place and give direction to her life.

One day she asked if she could go hiking with me. She'd been to a "sweat" and thought the Native American road to spiritual awareness might be for her. Somehow she had the idea that I was on that road, maybe because I took students on field trips to see the traces of Native American culture remaining in the rocks.

By then I'd more or less walked away from the whole "search," which, in my case, had never been very focused. I was reaching the conclusion that everything was probably fine, whether I got it or not. I tried to look at the trail as a trail, at hawks as hawks, the chance of seeing a cougar as a chance of seeing a cougar. I was beginning to get the idea that in life there are things we "do" and things we "are." Paying attention to the trail maybe all that was possible. I wasn't there yet. I still looked for signs and metaphors, I had yet to find the teacher who would help me with that, and a lot would happen in the meantime, but…

Christine showed up at the parking lot of Old Mission Dam wearing a pair of leggings and a T-shirt, carrying a water bottle. Our goal was the spot in Oak Canyon I called the "Indian Kitchen."

The "Indian Kitchen" is a fissure, a slit, through which a seasonal stream runs on its way to meet the San Diego River. The canyon is only twenty or thirty feet wide and a half a mile long. Some of the oldest rocks in the world line the canyon wall and, on the east side, make a flat floor where there are dozens of grinding holes and some carefully carved cisterns. In the narrowest part of the canyon, the local Kumeyaay Indians long ago pushed a couple of round boulders into the stream at strategic locations giving them a 12-month water supply in a secluded, defensible location. Pretty smart, I thought, compared to Father Junipero Serra's massive engineering project that resulted in the deaths of hundreds before it was finished. Oh well. That's a different story...

As we hiked, Christine told me all about her search and I listened wondering if she saw anything of what surrounded us. The trail has certain demands — the main one is "Pay attention." Then she asked, "What's the stick for?" I hiked with a stick that had been given to me by my friend Melanie for Christmas. Its name was "Old Gus" which is what I said I'd be called when I was old.

"Rattlesnakes," I said. "I pound the ground as I walk to let the snakes know I'm on the way, so they can move. And, if I see a snake in my way, I can use my stick to move it off the trail."

"Rattlesnakes?"

"Yeah."

"HERE????"

"Yeah." I was always surprised that people were surprised by that fact.

"Do you see them often?"

"No. The stick works. But seeing a snake in your way is a lot better than NOT seeing a snake in your way, right?"

Silence.

Then she went back to talking about God. I just listened. I was in front, responsible for the trail. Then, behind me, I heard a scream

"Aaaaa! Aaaa! AAAAA!!! Martha, HELP!"

Sounded like human for "Holy crap there's a snake!"

I stopped. I turned around. I saw Christine dancing and slapping and freaking out and screaming.

"Snake?" I asked.

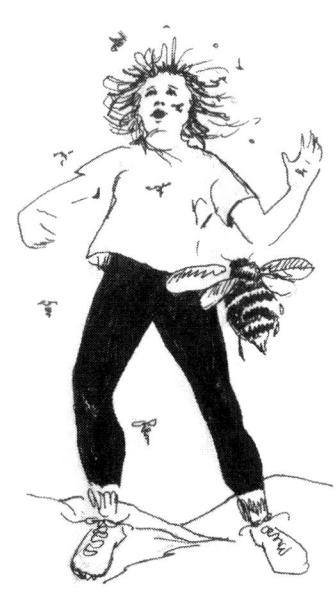

"No! Bees! I'm allergic!"

I saw hundreds of bees all around her. I'd walked through them, maybe stirred them up. Or maybe we intersected, I don't know. She'd walked into them. I reached for her and she took my hand. I pull her out of the swarm.

"I'm allergic. I could die."

"You're not going to die. Come on. Let's go."

"I can't go. I need to get home."

"OK, but where we are now forward is a shorter walk than back."

"How is that?"

"It's a loop. Come on. Up ahead I can fix your bee stings."

"I don't see how you can do that. Why did you bring me here?"

I didn't answer. That was the trail. Always different. Often surprising. People always want to go, but if they do, there's every chance they won't like it. I'd long stopped inviting people.

When we reached some loose dirt, I poured some water onto the dust and made mud. I knew the soil was full of salt, and it that it would help draw the poison out of Christine's bee stings.

"Here, take off your pants. We'll put some mud on the bee stings."

"Are you out of your mind?"

"It will work," I said.

Then Christine decided that probably I was right. She took off her leggings and both of us patted blobs of mud on the six or seven bee stings on her legs, then we put the poultice on the stings on her arms. "I'm going to go over there and sit on that rock and meditate," she said, "while the mud dries."

Relaxing was a very good plan, I thought, considering. Molly and I went to our usual spot and drank water and shared a granola bar.

In her skivvies, with black patches of mud on her legs and arms, Christine, in a full lotus position, sat on a higher rock, looking into the dark pool below hoping for a spiritual awakening. At a certain point, she called out that she saw an Indian's face silhouetted in the water.

"Cool," I said, "You want a granola bar?"

Just then I heard some happy whooping up the canyon. Mountain bikers. I knew they would fly past us to the fire road where they'd have to turn. I thought Christine might want to cover up.

"Hey, Christine, you might want to put your pants on. There are mountain bikers coming in a couple of minutes."

"How do you know that?"

I sighed.

She continued to sit, pondering, I guess, the face of the Indian she saw in the water. Then she saw them. She jumped up from her meditative spot and was heading back to me, back to her pants, at exactly the moment they came through. Seeing a nice looking woman wearing nothing but a t-shirt, bikini underwear and patches of black mud, two of the bikers crashed. The third laughed at them.

"Bee stings," I said to one of the fallen bikers. "Are you OK?"

"Yeah. I'm fine. I didn't expect… Well, never mind. Sorry." He blushed, then he and his buddy got back on their bikes and headed down the canyon. I heard them laughing.

Christine put on her leggings and we headed up and over the hill and back down to our cars, both of us silent on our return trip.

"How are the stings?" I asked when we got to the car.

"I think they're fine."

"Any dizziness? Do you want to go to the hospital?"

"No, I think I'm OK."

"Let me know when you get home?"

"I will."

***

Christine suffered no ill effects. Gossip in the school buzzed with the story of the bee stings, the mud, and the mountain bikers.

We were no closer to finding God, but we were no farther, either.

I wondered at the time about my friends' openly "spiritual" quests, the quest of the army of singing, snake-killing college students, and my own. All animals are looking for something when they leave their dens; coyotes for rabbits or fruit, rabbits for greens and fruit, hawks for snakes and rabbits, snakes for mice and baby squirrels and lizards. Still, even the master hunter, even a hawk, doesn't know if he's going to eat a rabbit, a mouse, a rattlesnake — or nothing. Because we have enough to eat, we human animals hunt for answers, and we sense nature has things to tell us. The problem with our searching is that we think we already know what nature has to say. We miss a lot in looking only for what we expect. I can't imagine a red-tail looking ONLY for a rabbit and ignoring the mice.

How many times have I tripped over *nothing* because I wasn't paying attention? *Island* by Aldous Huxley describes a jungle populated by birds whose natural cry sounds like, *"Here and now, boys, here and now."* Bees, snakes, hawks, flowers, hills, wind, water running over rocks, rocks themselves — all echo the same untranslated cry, trying to wake us up. Keep your eyes open, pound the ground in front of you, keep your dogs leashed and be aware — this moment, this red diamondback, is the only one of it there will ever be.

Dogs and Other Animals

Molly and I Go Skiing

"The first fall of snow is not only an event, but it is a magical event. You go to bed in one kind of world and wake up in another quite different, and if this is not enchantment, then where is it to be found?"
J.B. Priestley

Many of my dogs have been snow dogs — mostly Siberian Huskies, but Molly was an Australian Shepherd/Malamute mix. She was my first "snow dog," and she was very special. I think many dog owners have experienced life with an extraordinary dog, and Molly was just such a one.

Around Valentine's Day in 1989, I found her in a big cardboard box with her brothers and sisters at the El Cajon swap meet. Her mom was a Malamute. The people were very eager to get rid of the pups. It appeared that they'd hoped to breed Malamutes, but a licentious Aussie had gotten to her first. The pups were free, somewhere between 6 and 8 weeks old.

It was, for me, love at first sight. Molly was patterned like a blue merle Aussie. Her eyes were brown and she had a little pink heart shape on her nose. She was born without a tail — just a little flap of fur where a tail would have been. I hadn't thought of having two dogs, but Truffle had recently been spayed and maybe she would look at Molly as her own pup.

The very first day — that very afternoon — I took her to the Laguna Mountains with Truffle, hiking. She was far too small for that, but it gave me my first glimpse into her amazing mind. Tiny as she was, when she got hot and tired, she found a shady place and dug with her little feet until she found cool, damp earth and she laid down, flat on her belly, and looked up at me.

I became very familiar with that look. It said, "Surely you know better than this?"

And she smiled.

I ended up carrying her out, realizing how dumb — and inadvertently cruel — I had been.

Her nickname became "Smiler" for the way she had of curling back her lips when she was overjoyed happy to see the people she loved. With no tail to wag, she had to do something.

Molly didn't bark; she "woo-woo"ed. She went to puppy school and dropped out. Once she felt she'd mastered a skill such as "sit" or "down" she just went to sleep. She did take the final exam and passed with flying colors. Throughout her life, she never walked well on a leash; neither of the breeds in her ancestry was exactly what you'd call "submissive."

When tested with sheep, she showed no interest in herding, but she would keep my niece and her little friends in one corner of the backyard when she was tired of playing with them. Molly had intelligence and will, and, from her, I learned how a human and a dog can be partners, friends, equals. That particular balance became my goal in my relationship with all the dogs in my life.

We lived together for nearly fifteen years. They were tumultuous years in my life, but Molly stayed the course with her particular fierce and light-hearted sense of how things should be.

Most of all, we wanted to be together ALL THE TIME. We loved each other fiercely.

***

One March afternoon in 2000 I was at work and heard the news that more than 20 inches of snow had fallen in the Laguna Mountains and was expected to continue — at a slower rate — all night.

I wanted to ski. I found, to my great surprise, that there was a place in San Diego where I could rent X-country skis. I called and said, "I need skis, boots, and poles, whatever, for a woman 5'2" 160 pounds, 7.5 shoes. Can I come and get them this afternoon?"

"Yeah, sure. You know where we are?"

"Not really." He gave me directions. I made my plans known to my bosses (who were also colleagues) that I would not be at school/work the next day, and that I would call in sick. I explained that I was going skiing with my dog. There in San Diego County I was going to have a "snow day."

"Isn't that dangerous? To ski alone like that in the backcountry?"

A common question in my life. I knew people — friends — who did really dangerous things. I was just going to the nearby mountains to X-country ski with my best friend who happened to be a dog. In the Laguna Mountains, there was zero chance of an avalanche. There really was NOTHING dangerous about it unless I fell and broke something. I believed (on some level) that Molly was perfectly capable of rescuing me and driving home.

I walked in the shop and the guy behind the counter — the owner — looked up and said, "5'2" 160?"

"Yep."

"Here you go. Try on the boots."

The boots were fine.

I was on fire with excitement. I was rapturous. I had not X-country skied in YEARS, maybe a DECADE. I couldn't wait. I was going skiing. *Snow!!!!* The next morning Molly and I were on the road loud music blasting out of the CD player.

I planned to park at the Meadows Information Station on the Sunrise Highway. I hoped the road weren't closed. I didn't have chains. I figured if the road were closed I'd park where I could and just ski up the road with my dog on a leash, but on that holy day, we got lucky. Waaa—HOOO!

I had no plan, no route. I was just going to ski. I knew the snow would be great. Some of the best X-country skiing in my life was in Southern California, dense snow, receptive to skis, easy to break trail, easy to turn, and fast on hills.

I buckled on Molly's pack so she could carry our water and granola bars, and we were off across the meadow and then down, down to Laguna Pond.

About 50 feet above Laguna Pond the season changed to spring. The warmer air, coming from the ocean laden with water, was here soft mist bending to the cool surface of the pond on its way to higher, colder elevations where it would turn to snow. In those mountains, the Lagunas, the seasons are often inches from each other. I have stood on a trail on the northeast side of the Lagunas, over the desert, arms outstretched, one hand in a winter storm and the other in sunshine, the climate created by the rain shadow.

I turned and we skied back up to winter then down again to spring, and up and then, having enjoyed the phenomenon enough, I returned to winter to stay. There we climbed hills and skied down, and the snow fell. On the top of one hill above the meadow, Molly jumped up and landed on her back. She rolled around, making angels in the deep snow. I stepped out of my skis and got down beside her to made an angel of my own. When I finished, I looked over at my blissful, wet, snowy dog and saw her…

Smiling.

Molly and I Chase the Sky

A certain hermit once said, "There is one thing that even I, who have no worldly entanglements, would be sorry to give up; the beauty of the sky.

The Tsurezcuregusa of Kenko, Essays in Idleness

Not long ago, on a glorious December afternoon here in the San Luis Valley of Colorado, I was walking with Dusty T. Dog, my Dobie/Lab mix, and Polar Bear Yeti T. Dog, my Akbash. I was enjoying the stiff, cool breeze and the early winter light, I remembered another day December day, maybe sixteen years ago…

It started out a normal hike about 9 am at The Meadows Information Station turn-out on the Sunrise Highway in the Laguna Mountains. I just wanted to go hiking with Molly. I didn't know for sure where we'd hike or anything, but I was going to enjoy the clear windy day with my best friend.

I'd brought lunch — yogurt, granola bars, a couple of dog cookies and a soda — and water. There was a good well at what I imagined would be our halfway point where I could refill our water and Molly could have a good, long drink if she wanted.

We hit the trail. The Laguna Mountains are 7000+ feet in elevation, the highest in San Diego County. Along the northeast rim, they drop nearly straight down to the desert.

Some of the trails go through forests of Jeffery Pine. Others go through manzanita scrub. There are meadows and streams and waterfalls and man-made dams that form "lakes" (big ponds).

Molly

There was an unbelievably blue sky. Every familiar turning looked new, scoured with wind-washed light. The silvery clouds seemed close enough to touch.

We climbed up Garnet Peak and ate lunch, then came back down, ran across the road and down the Noble Canyon trail, past the most amazing grandfather manzanita, to Indian Springs, back up, returned to the well for the third time, then found our way to the Sunset Trail again to return to the car.

As we crossed the meadow, the last bit before reaching the end of the trail, my feet hurt on top and on the bottom. There was one painless moment in between footfall and foot lift. It was dark. We'd been hiking for 8 hours.

We hiked 26 miles on that glorious day. When we finished, it was dark, and we were both starving.

I've hiked in the Alps, the Dolomites, the Cinque Terre and in Arizona, Oregon, Montana, Wyoming, Utah and Colorado. I even made it most of the way up a Chinese mountain, but that was the best hike of my life, chasing the beauty of the sky with Molly.

Ariel, the Deer and Riddley Walker

Dint see no other dogs jus only him. Looking at me and wagging his tail slow. Then he ternt and gone off easy looking back over his sholder like he wantit me to foller so I follert.

　　　　　　　　　　　　　　　　Russell Hoban, Riddley Walker

　　Once in a while a book will capture me, and I was captured by *Riddley Walker* by Russell Hoban. It's science fiction, set in a post-apocalyptic England. The apocalypse was the result of nuclear war, so one of the governing motifs in the novel is atomic energy.

　　Hoban devised a fractured but recognizable English for this novel. It's difficult enough to be intriguing, but not so difficult that it impedes immersion in the story.

　　I didn't want to put the book down even though my dogs were clamoring for a hike. Particularly Ariel. In *Riddley Walker* dogs — no longer domesticated — have special intelligence that humans don't have, maybe never had, maybe lost as they have lost much of their knowledge.

　　Ariel was a low-content wolf/husky hybrid. She scared people once in a while when her lupine appearance converged with their ignorance. She was much smaller than a wolf, and she had a blue eye. When I first got her, she would escape whenever she got the chance. After a while, she learned that <u>not</u> running off meant she'd get to go hiking and she'd get to be with me. Over time, this beautiful, half-wild, creature who'd never had a real home or a real person, fell passionately in love with me. She was a one-woman dog, and a great hiking pal, always. I felt honored.

Ariel was a dog from *Riddley Walker*, not quite tame.

I leashed her (she had to be leashed on the trail) and off we went.

It was a *Riddley Walker* day, as close to English weather as anyone could ever find in the chaparral of Southern California. It had been raining off and on, settling the dust on the trail without making mud. The fog tangled in the oak trees at the bottom of Suycott Wash and it reached toward the tops of the two Fortuna Mountains. I had a narrow ridge trail in mind, a wild semi-secret link between two main trails.

Ariel on the Garnet Peak Trail, Laguna Mountains, Winter 2004

We hiked embraced by the fragrance of damp black sage. Suddenly I got the feeling that we were being watched. I turned. On a hill, about 50 yards behind us, was a very alert mule deer doe.

"Did you see her, Ariel?" But I knew she had. We reached the high spot in the hike, a rise from which I could see down a trail toward a pond, back through the wash and up to the mountain. Mists swirled around us. I looked at Ariel and thought, "What if?" I loosened my hold on her leash so she was not obliged to heel. She looked at me and somehow got the message that I was reversing our roles. She could lead me.

Ariel walked purposefully, with her nose in the air. We went around our hill on foot paths belonging to coyote, deer, and fox. We walked straight down and onto the main trail, then we turned into thicket of sumac and willow. Ariel stopped.

There, within arm's reach, was the doe looking straight into my eyes. Ariel had made *Riddley Walker* come true.

Three Guys on the PCT

"Occasionally, he would exclaim over a view or regard with admiration some passing marvel of nature, but mostly to him hiking was a tiring, dirty, pointless slog between distantly spaced comfort zones."
                                    Bill Bryson, <u>A Walk in the Woods</u>

I hiked the Pacific Crest Trail. No, really, I did. No, wait. I hiked ON the PCT. I had dreams. Dreams are not enough. I had but one car and no reliable hiking buddy, so there I was, hiking the PCT in increments (both directions) covering, finally, fifteen or twenty miles (twice). At that point, I needed to find a friend with a car if I were going to continue to make this a weekend, *deja-vu* inch-worm kind of hike. And then, by the time I got north of Julian, an hour or so drive, I wouldn't be able to be a *deja-vu* inch-worm anymore.

Oh well. A hike's a hike and it was never — for me — about getting anywhere. I didn't have that kind of time or money. Most of my hikes had to take place in the hours after school (for one semester I was lucky to have time before school) and on weekends. Sometimes I was traveling away from home, and I hiked something else. It was always the paired passions — motion and vision.

One of my favorite hikes was up the Garnet Peak Trail in the Laguna Mountains. Most often I began at the Penny Pines pull out on the Sunrise Highway.

Over the years I lived in San Diego I hiked that trail at least a hundred times. From the top, you can see FAR, way out to the Salton Sea and way out to the San Bernardinos, the snow-covered peaks of San Gorgornio and San Jacinto. For this perpetually homesick Colorado girl, that was WONDERFUL. Not only that, but the drop off on the north side of Garnet Peak is spectacular. The peak itself is 5900 feet, but on the northeast side, it drops down straight to the desert floor which is sea level or below.

Once I even cross-country skied up that mountain. There was plenty of snow, but nowhere to plant poles except in 20-inch tall Manzanita scrub. It was laughable — and fun.

Most of the trail to Garnet Peak is the PCT. At a certain point, the PCT intersects the up-the-mountain trail and a hiker turns to a steep up-hill. One late afternoon several years ago I was hiking back to the car with Ariel after enjoying some time on the top. I ran into a guy about my age, mid-fifties. He was perky and happy and striding along purposefully. He looked like a very fit guy from New York, doctor or lawyer, dark eyes, black glasses, graying goatee. He had new gear, only slightly broken in, and he used his trekking poles as if they were best friends. "Hi!" he said, stopping.

"Hi," I said, also stopping. Having noticed his equipment I had to ask, "Are you doing the PCT?"

"Trying, me and my two buddies." I heard in his voice that he WAS from New York. "You'll run into them. Do you know anything about the Pioneer Mail Campground?"

"It's nice, good water, real toilets but no showers, lots of space to pitch a tent. It's mainly used as a picnic area."

"From there? Do you know?"

I did. "Yeah. After that, you'll head uphill again — from here it's downhill to Pioneer Mail. There's a section where you can't see much but rocks and manzanita on both sides of the trail, then you turn a corner and look out over the desert. Very dramatic. Two or three miles out from Pioneer Mail on the PCT, closer on the road. Then there is a spot where people like to hang-glide."

"Thanks. I'd better keep moving. Sun's about down. Is it far?"

"Thirty minutes to an hour, I'd say, depending. Like I said, it's downhill. Good luck!"

I continued, enjoying the pinkish glow of after-sunset light. It wasn't long before I ran into the second guy, heavier-set, not as neatly packed as the first guy or as obviously on a mission — happy in an easy-going kind of way. His gear looked more used.

"Did you see my buddy up ahead?"

"Yeah, he's really moving."

"That's what he does." The man smiled a friendly smile. "Sure is beautiful up here. You live here?"

"Not far. I live in a small town about 15 miles away in the Cuyamacas, the next mountain range to the west."

"Just about paradise, I'd say. I'd better get moving. Campground's up ahead?"

"About an hour."

"It'll be dark. Nothing like setting up a tent in the dark." He chuckled.

"That's for sure. Good luck!"

It was quite a while — nearly dark — before I encountered the third guy. He was carrying his mattress in one hand. He was wearing untied sneakers. His pack was open at the top. His face was red.

"Hi," I said.

"I hate this," he said. "Have you seen my buddies up there? They couldn't even wait."

"Yeah, one's way up there, then there's one a little ways ahead. You could catch up."

"Like hell."

"Good luck," I said, not wanting to laugh in front of him, and moved on.

Hard to say who of those three would make it and who would not. It didn't look good for the last guy — I figured he'd bail out in the nearest town, Julian. In fact, I was surprised he didn't ask me for a ride. The other two? Well, the second guy seemed happy and easy-going enough for the first one not to get on his nerves.

I thought there was hope.

The Santa Ana

"Heaven and earth are ruthless"

Lao Tse, <u>Tao Te Ching</u>

In 2003 the biggest fire in the history of California (to date; sadly since there has been an even larger fire) burned a total of 280,000 acres — part of it through the cities and to the coast. Since that event, California has changed its policies for fighting wildfires, including using more controlled burns and ramping up its ability to respond. It was named The Cedar Fire.

I had lived in my stone house in Descanso -- my dream home -- for a full five weeks. I'd moved out of the hood and up there to be closer to the mountains and higher altitude hiking. For those weeks I spent my time trying to figure out my new life in my new house, moving in psychically and physically.

On October 25, 2003, I was finally ready for a real hike, so Ariel and I went up to the Lagunas to hike the Garnet Peak trail.

It was a splendid fall day. October is often one of the most miserable and hottest months in San Diego County. That day we were getting a break from the heat. Ariel and I hit the trail about 3 pm, just right to reach the top of the mountain to watch the sun fade in the West and see the Salton Sea and the Anza Borrego Desert respond with their changing colors.

It was, for me, the magic hour.

There was a breeze, cool and sweet, making the air just the right temperature. We were sitting on top of the mountain, drinking water and enjoying our granola bars, when suddenly there was an immense "Whoosh!" from the valley floor up the face of the mountain followed by a BANG, as loud as an explosion, literally right next to me.

A Santa Ana had hit the mountain. I was amazed, thrilled, by the experience. I went back down only thinking that now that I lived up there I would be able to experience more of the reality of these strange, wild Southern California Coastal Mountains.

The wind blew hard all night -- in time I would experience harder winds, some blasting 70 mph down my street -- but this was still something.

The next day I decided to paint my bathroom. I used some paint I found in the shed and painted designs on the wall from towels some good friends had given me. I went ahead and painted my name on my mailbox -- with shamrocks as decorations. The wind blew branches from the trees and the sky was a perfect blue.

When I finished I decided to go to town, to Alpine, to get things for my bathroom -- a bath brush, fancy soap, that kind of stuff. As I crested the hill to drop into town I saw fire. Somehow my mind blotted the reality of it out of my consciousness, and I bought things at the Rite-Aid as if there was nothing strange going on down the road or across the highway.

After that, I was fixated on the mountains to the west of my house -- between me and San Diego -- and the cloud of smoke that my mind insisted on turning into just a cloud. I had no radio so I listened in the truck.

The Santa Ana was blowing the fire into San Diego; neighborhoods had been burned. People had been killed. It was moving very fast, 5000 acres an hour. It would reach the ocean.

The night sky looked as if someone had put masking tape across it. One side was black, clear, starlit. The other side was smoke. Early the next morning, the wind shifted. The Sant Ana was over and the wind was blowing inland, toward the mountains. At four am, the sheriff drove up and down the meandering, tangled streets of my town. "You are ordered to evacuate. Go to Mountain Empire High School. There is a Red Cross Evacuation Shelter. Repeat, You are ordered to evacuate. Go to Mountain Empire High school." There was a pause, then, "Good luck." All sounding like the voice of doom.

I had packed ahead of the evacuation, but the only valuables I took were my four dogs, their food, food for me, camping equipment, water and the *Rubaiyat of Omar Khayyam* my dad had given me the last Christmas he was alive, a book he'd carried in the war.

When I looked west, toward the cloud of smoke, I could see the red glow of flames coming toward my town.

We spent the night in the truck in a parking lot at the not-so-local-local high school and the day in a park in Pine Valley. When the highway into San Diego was finally safe to drive, I drove down to stay with friends. There was fire on both sides of the freeway.

When it was over, I had been away from home for a week.

The drive back up the mountain was stupefying. All the hills were black with occasional splotches of orange flame retardant. Many hills were smoldering. Where firefighters had saved homes and businesses there were hastily made signs saying, "Thank you, firefighters!" The computer operated illuminated sign of Viejas Outlet Mall and Casino was dark, but in a couple of days it would say, "Thank You Firefighters." That message would remain for nearly a year.

On my way up home, I passed dozens of fire trucks from all over the United States, Wyoming, Colorado, Texas, Oregon. I wept.

The fire burned the southernmost rainforest in North America in which stood the southernmost indigenous redwood trees.

It was not until December that the fires were all out. Driving through the Cuyamaca Mountains for the next couple of months meant driving through a blackened, smoldering Hellish landscape.

But...*Nature*. Nature never gives up.

Rain that winter came fast and hard. The river through my town boiled down from the mountains black with ash. Never was the winter sky more blue than in the winter of 2003/2004. Never did the remaining golden grass glow so fervently. Never did the bald eagles living around Lake Cuyamaca fish so passionately or successfully. Redwood seeds -- that need fire to germinate -- expanded in the sandy soil fertilized by ash. In the midst of all that was wrong, struggling and homeless people and the loss of human life, the mountains themselves were preparing the next big forest.

The fire stopped on the Garnet Peak Trail exactly where the previous fire had diminished the available fuel. Ariel and I returned to the trail throughout the winter and spring, watching the Manzanita scrub grow back from the roots where burned trees stood like sticks of vine charcoal against the parchment of snow.

Morning

"Morning is when I am awake and there is a dawn in me".
Henry David Thoreau, <u>Walden</u>

    Everyone knows that the best time to see animals is in the early morning or at dusk. As most of my hiking life overlapped the years of my teaching life, and I usually taught early morning classes, my only chance was dusk. But there was one semester when my first class was at one pm. If I were going to hike at all that semester, I had to get out early. I adapted to this and got up and out so I could get back and shower in time to drive down the mountain to the university for a 1 pm class. I only had an hour more or less on the trail.

    My first morning hike that winter led me to a very different world than I'd known in my late afternoon ramblings. Freezing temperatures and ocean fog had left pale frost on the trees. The fog stretched erratically up the valleys and I could read its movement in its "frost prints." The morning was magical, silent, frost-softened, cold, gray and dull green, shadows and promise.

The Models — Jasmine and Lily — and I walked through the first part of the hike, a part I called "the enchanted forest," and then around a huge rocky outcrop, behind the eerie ridge and then up the hill toward the pond.

There she was.

She stopped in the first moment of downhill lope. She had long legs, big feet, a nub of a tail. She was the color of the rocks and frost shadows all around us. She looked intently at The Models and me, curious and wary.

"Hello, Bob," I said, but silently. "You are beautiful. I'm glad to see you."

I felt a little tingle in my spine. I had forgotten all the creatures with whom I shared those trails. I had forgotten her. This was not just a circuit on which I walked the dogs. This was someone's home. Inside myself, I thanked her for reminding me. My hiking at the same time every day meant the wild things knew where I was and when. Changing my clock changed their world.

She stood there a long time. The Models sat, and I stood without moving. I wasn't going to bother her or startle her or take away her trail or race her to the pond. Finally, she darted off down the hill.

I saw her again some weeks later. She crossed the trail a few feet in front of me carrying a rabbit in her mouth. I guessed she had kittens. My heart saluted her.

Spirit Guide?

And I think in this empty world there was room for me and a mountain lion.

D. H. Lawrence, "Mountain Lion"

In the late 1980s, about the time I got my first dog, Truffle and discovered Mission Trails Regional Park and began hiking in the chaparral. I was confused inside. My marriage was disappointing. I was not making any progress in my career. I was writing, but what? Mostly letters to people who lived in the same city. An important ingredient (satisfaction?) was missing from my life. I filled that emptiness with hiking through a landscape haunted by Indians.

There were grinding holes in the rocks around me; there was an ingenious a dam they built to hold water throughout the year; cuts and wearing of rocks along a stream showed a place where they may have turned the yucca into fibers for rope and sandals; the stands of oak at the end of a canyon gave them their staple food; the stream and river were lined with willows they used for houses and storage. Hiking in Mission Trails and reading *The Seven Arrows* inspired me to look for my spirit animal. I got my wish, in a scary, beautiful journey.

It began with a dream I had in Montana while visiting my mom. In the dream, my mom, husband and I were driving on the highway out of Red Lodge heading up to Beartooth Summit. From my back seat window, I saw a mountain lion. I spoke up, but both of them said, "Oh don't be silly. There is no mountain lion. What would a mountain lion be doing so close to the road?"

After that, dreams of cougars recurred frequently. In one, I was on the road from Julian to the Laguna Mountains, north of Lake Cuyamaca, crossing pasture land. A mountain lion was attacking a herd of cattle. It noticed me by the fence and came to me. I was frightened and drove away. It chased my car. I drove a red Ford Escort, even though, in life, I had a truck. The Escort came a few years later, after my mom died.

In another, a mountain lion came to my front yard in City Heights to tell me that my mom was an alcoholic. The cougar told me I should not give up my life to care for my mom. I had this dream more than four years before I learned that, for many years, my mother had been a secret alcoholic.

Not all the dreams were prescient, but all were beautiful. In one dream, a cougar led me to rescue a hawk that had been blown down in a storm. In others, they walked beside me on the trails of mystical hikes in impossible landscapes, the Swiss Alps, years before I thought of going to Switzerland.

I did some research into the significance of a mountain lion as a spirit animal and learned that its gift is balance, their graceful leaps suspended by their long, heavy tail. I painted a life-sized cougar on the inside of the topper of my 1988 Ford Ranger, the focal point of a mural of rocks, sky and hawks. My friends called it the "Sistine Camper." When I changed phone companies, and they asked what number I wanted, I asked for p-u-m-a, not realizing those had been the digits in my mom's phone number.

In 1993 I began slipping into a mental crisis. One of the first signs was too wonderful to call insanity. I awoke in the night to see a cougar beside my bed, haloed with ultramarine light. He was watching me sleep. I wanted to touch him, but lay paralyzed. That he was the advance "man" for madness didn't occur to me. One symptom of mania is that kind of hallucination, and the feeling of a deep, personal connection to the divine essence.

I had seen his tracks three times in real life. The first time in California, skiing on Cuyamaca Mountain in 1985. The second, skiing in the Beartooths in Montana; the third in the chaparral dust at Mission Trails. I was almost satisfied with that, the confirmation that he prowled where I prowled, but deep inside I wanted more. I began hiking at dusk into dark with the dim hope of encountering a mountain lion.

Then, in the Cuyamaca Mountains near San Diego, there were several deadly cougar attacks on people. It's true that one of the women killed was hiking with a bloody steak in her backpack (hardly the cougar's fault that she smelled like fresh food) but there was a heightened sense of danger all around the mountains. A ranger in the Lagunas pulling in a garden hose at the ranger station found a full-grown, female cougar playing with the end of it, just like the household cat. It should have been beautiful and amusing to the ranger, but because of the deaths, the ranger was scared. Then one of my friends canceled a hike with me because a cougar had been sighted at Mission Trails. I heard her on my cell phone say, "I suppose you WANT to go and you think I'm a coward." Well, I did want to go, and I thought she was selfish. The likelihood of our seeing the cougar was minimal; the possible reward incredible. I went without her.

I didn't give up.

I'd learned from my years hiking in the chaparral that wonderful things happen when you inject your presence into the wild clock. In my hikes at Mission Trails a pair of red-tails learned that when I arrived — at about the same time every day — my dogs would help them hunt by chasing critters out from under bushes. They perched on the same boulder every afternoon waiting for the dogs. I often hiked with these birds flying beside me close enough that, as I hiked the top of a ridge, I could see their eyes, their feathers, their mouths, the motion of their tails.

I normally hiked alone, or with dogs, and sometimes people on a trail asked me if I were frightened. I said I was more afraid NOT to hike than to hike alone. I really didn't have a choice. Even with a few friends to hike with, most hikes were solitary. As a nod to the danger, I attached to my key ring one of the little goat bells I'd brought back from Zürich. It was an idiot warning system since I made sure it was completely muffled when I hiked.

When I moved up to the Cuyamacas, I was able to hike daily in the Lagunas, "real" mountains. A three mile hike when I didn't have much time, and a longer hike, between 8 and 12 miles, if I had the time. The short hike became a morning hike, and the long hike later in the afternoon so the day cooled off as I tired. In my morning hikes, I often crossed tracks with a bobcat as she went for a drink, caught a squirrel or headed up a hill after visiting the pond. Late afternoon was all about feral cattle, rattlesnakes, ground squirrels, and, occasionally, coyotes. The afternoon light was beautiful, the air was soft, and I had no complaints about anything. Often, at either time, I caught sight of deer.

About 6 p.m. on August 4, 2004, I was walking back from Lake Laguna down a small slope toward the pond. In front of me, about 50 feet, I noticed a shadowy shape moving against the rocks. The sun was in my eyes making it difficult to see. I lifted my hand to shade my eyes. The animal stopped and crouched very much like a house cat caught doing something it shouldn't. For a moment I couldn't really SEE what I SAW. The reality of it struggled to penetrate a brain that had waited so long. Then I knew what's — whose! — silhouette it was. I stopped, Ariel beside me.

I spoke aloud to the cat. "I have wanted to see you for a long time, but that's all I want, so please just turn and go back into those rocks until I get past you." She looked toward me and then turned around and went into the rocks. Ariel and I continued, facing the rocks constantly, you can be sure. 30 feet on the other side, I stopped to see the mountain lion sitting on top of the outcropping looking at me.

It was then I realized I had been a part of her world for a couple of years. Because my hike that day was later than usual, our paths had crossed.

***

2004 was the last year I was able to hike the way I had been hiking for most of my life. As the weather cooled, I began having problems I'd never had before. My back and quads were increasingly painful as I walked. More and more often, a short hike felt like a long one. I had to lift my right leg into my truck, and when I got out, I had a very hard time standing up straight and walking to the house.

In November I was on the floor of my house, poking the fire in my wood stove to re-energize the coals when the phone rang, my landline. I could not get up to answer. I crawled across the floor and pulled myself up using the door jam to the kitchen. I missed the call. From there was the long slow process of misdiagnoses, physical therapy, and months of excruciating pain before the discovery of osteoarthritis in my hip. This was caused by trail running and a lifetime of sports injuries. I had hip resurfacing surgery in 2007. My hip is now as good as new, but I have changed.

Only very recently have I understood what happened that day in August. I see that moment now as a perfect benediction.

If You Have a Dog, You Don't Need a Guru

"Dogs are our link to paradise... To sit with a dog on a hillside on a glorious afternoon is to be back in Eden, where doing nothing was not boring--it was peace."

Milan Kundera

One of the places I sometimes walked with my dogs is Lake Murray. It's a man-made lake, one of the reservoirs built to provide drinking water for San Diego. It's a very nice place to go. There are picnic tables and restrooms and fireworks on the 4th of July. It's very popular among San Diegans and every summer evening you can find joggers of all ages, walkers with and without dogs, families having picnics or fishing, bicyclists and sometimes even the elusive rollerblader. The three-mile one way (six miles to go the whole way, turn around and return) "trail" is nicely paved and marked with distances in 1/2 mile intervals. I went there once in a while on summer evenings when I just wanted to walk and not deal with snakes I couldn't see, or rocks or roots or all the things connected with back-country trails.

It is a great place to watch people. I liked imagining the stories behind the faces I saw, stories that explained why they were making their lake circuits, striding, so many spandex embraced recruits toward a sign that says, "It doesn't count if you don't touch HIT the fence." I don't know what "it" is and I never hit the sign, but people are like that, whatever goal, whatever target, they want to reach it. There was a very attractive, petite brunette who pounded the pavement to the two-mile marker, that far, no farther and never less. "I'm doing to do my four miles and I'm going to turn around, go home and cook dinner." That was the story I made up for her.

I was no different. Once I got to the point where I was walking the whole way (rehabbing from a knee injury) I almost hated myself if, for any reason, I didn't go that far. Five instead of six miles seemed a negation, "anti-exercise." I think this was the story of a lot of people at Lake Murray, but my dogs were having no part of it.

"Come ON!" I'd yell at Truffle or Kelly or Lupo or Molly as they lagged behind to smell something, look at the bushes move, or stare at a wandering duck.

My dog Molly had been conditioned to notice hawks in flight. While there are very few things I'd rather see than a hawk, when Molly stopped dead still one day as a Cooper's Hawk flew low behind me, I became impatient because, dammit! We had to MOVE.

Her stubbornness forced me to turn around — with the thought of issuing a militaristic reprimand — but when I turned, I saw the bird, his wings brushing the chaparral, his beak pointed into a gully where he had seen a mouse. Awakened by my dog, I waited: I knew he would come back to the tree from which he had made his dive.

As I waited, I noticed the light; bits of sun scattered on the lake surface. Hysterical ducks ridiculed me from the shadows of the reeds. Molly came suddenly to attention, ears cocked forward, her eyes seeming to physically penetrate the space between us and the hawk that Molly sensed, but which I could not yet see. Suddenly, there he was above me, holding "rodent-to-go" in his claws. Still, he somehow managed to land on a branch where he ate, rending and tearing the mouse and gulping down the bits, all picturesquely silhouetted against the setting sun. I watched it all; it was something I had never seen before. People passed, marched, ran, skated and biked around me.

Lupo Dreams of Rabbits

By the time he finished, I had to leave. I had only walked a mile, but once again I'd learned a lesson from a dog. For years I'd watched my dogs running through the brush, Lupo chasing a rabbit, Truffle flushing quail out from under the white sage, Kelly watching lizards, all of them sometimes just sitting there, apparently doing nothing. When they saw a puddle, they swam; when there were tadpoles to chase, water-skippers to watch, they fished. Wherever they were, they were THERE.

I realized that afternoon just how limited I am by my ideas of things; I think I know what I'm doing. Like other people, I have a "purpose" in life and the purpose is usually in the future, something I will reach when we "hit the fence." That afternoon it struck me that it's often when we hit the fence that we realize that we didn't stop enough along the way. After that, I began to SEE Lake Murray, the ospreys, the cormorants, the children and every other thing I had ignored. And, Molly's lesson stuck.

Now, I'm less mobile — but mobile enough for a long dog walk through my town, or in a field or seasonally closed golf course or a reasonably flat trail. I can't do downhills easily, but I do them. Knowing that I don't have to "go the whole way or it's a negation," I can stop to let Bear roll in a patch of snow, wait for little, old Mindy, my Aussie, who walks so slowly. I can celebrate Dusty's joy when I call him back to me and he comes running like it's the best thing that ever happened to him. I can stop and notice the changing light on the bark of the young aspen tree, the emerging buds of leaves that are yet two months away. I can see the shadows of branches as the sun hits the golden-leafed cottonwood from a November angle. I can look up through the cottonwood branches and notice the pale ultramarine blue of the sky when it's covered with a fine veil of cloud. I can follow a dog who follows a scent.

There is really nothing I love more than being out in the wind with my dogs on any kind of day, endeavoring not to go anywhere, but just to be with them, as they are.

Thank you, Molly.

Snakes

"When I write 'paradise' I mean not only apple trees and golden women but also scorpions and tarantulas and flies, rattlesnakes and Gila monsters, sandstorms, volcanoes and earthquakes, bacteria and bear, cactus, yucca, bladderweed, ocotillo and mesquite, flash floods and quicksand…"
Edward Abbey, <u>Desert Solitaire</u>

In my Spirit Animal seeking days, I covered a lot of miles. Along with improving my odds of seeing a cougar, all this mileage improved my chances of seeing a lot of other things. Rattlesnakes were common enough that I called them, "snake *du jour*." I knew I'd see one before a three-hour hike was over, but believed (based on experience) that two snake sightings were unlikely. They are somewhat territorial, as well, and I got so I knew where on which trail I could expect to see one. I liked seeing them at the beginning of a hike and getting their bone-chilling beauty out of the way.

I've probably seen a thousand rattlesnakes -- maybe the same one over and over -- but easily a thousand "sightings." The first time was in 1988. I was with my dog, Truffle. We were not yet able to make it to the top of Big Dog Health and Fitness Spa when we saw our first snake.

Truffle was a 10-month-old pup. I was a chubby, out-of-shape woman of 36. We were going along in our own inimitable way, and suddenly I heard it. I knew exactly what it was even though it was the first time. I screamed. Truffle jumped. I grabbed her. We ran down the hill to the car.

I called my mom and told her, "The only good snake stick is a 22!"

She was terrified of snakes because of their preponderance in the Montana prairie where she grew up, but to my surprise, she did not agree. "He wasn't in your backyard, was he?"

"No."

"Were you in his?"

That pretty much defined and firmed up my attitude toward rattlesnakes. Snakes do a lot of good work out there in the wild. It was my job to watch where I was going.

Truffle and I returned to hike the hill the next day, going up with added vigilance. There was the snake in the same place. It was a small rattlesnake, only 12 inches long. A Mojave Diamondback, grey/brown and white/tan. When it rattled, Truffle turned so fast she pulled the leash out of my hand and ran, hell-bent, to the car. One experience had taught that dog that when you hear a rattlesnake, your human screams, and you run back to the car…

I'd planned to keep going, but I had to get my dog.

**

Over time, I began to feel a kind of fondness for rattlesnakes. I realized that they were easily frightened and had an active desire NOT to bite anything that was not food. A rattlesnake's life is focused on two questions, "Food? Not food?"

I developed a general way of observing the lower parts of bushes as I walked, and most of the time I saw snakes before I reached them. Sometimes a snake would be lying across a trail. Once in a while, the trail might be too narrow for me to feel comfortable crossing in front of the snake's sharp end, but for those situations I carried a long walking stick.

My closest call was during a moment of "relaxed vigilance." My mind was on other things.

Late one afternoon on an easy trail across a chaparral meadow with two dogs. One was Mathilda, young, frisky, sheltie/chow mix, who was way too eager to meet everyone. I noticed a couple of mountain bikers coming toward us, about 50 feet away, so I quickly moved off the trail with the dogs and instantly heard a buzz. I looked down to see a young rattlesnake about four inches from Mathilda's nose. Without even thinking about it, I took my walking stick and put it between the snake and Mathilda. I shook the stick. Frightened, the snake leaned backward and then moved away, pure reflex.

The snake gone, I looked up, thinking the bikers had to have passed by then, but they had not even moved 10 feet.

Time had stopped.

***

One of the most interesting moments I had with a rattlesnake involved a ground squirrel. She was on the side of the road with three little baby ground squirrels — perfect snake food. A young rattlesnake was coiled right in front of the mother squirrel, a foot away, in striking distance. Mom had made herself as big as she could. Her tail was up, fluffed to maximum fluffiness. Her little ones, about a finger long, each of them, crouched behind her. I just stood there and watched. What ferocity and determination both in that little squirrel and in that hungry snake. After about twenty minutes, the snake backed away.

He could have taken down the mom. She was possible dinner, too, but he didn't. He just left, retreated to the undergrowth. I figured that for that snake ground squirrels were like buses; there'd be another one along shortly.

***

I expected to see a rattlesnake every day I hiked during snake season — February to mid-November. Most of the snakes I saw were rattlesnakes, but not all. Once I picked up a sweet rosy boa at the beginning of my hike, put her in the pocket of my cargo shorts, hiked with her for an hour or so then put her back where I'd found her. I don't know why I did that. It just seemed like a good idea at the time.

Another time I was hiking on a ridge. A large bird flying overhead dropped a snake. It happened to land on my trail. I found it, a rosy boa, stunned but all right. It was a little freaky to think that some airborne predator could drop a rattlesnake on me, but what were the odds?

I seldom saw the beautiful black and yellow California king snakes or gopher snakes, but I knew they were around from their tracks in the dust. Rattlesnakes have particular belly scales, a lot like bulldozer wheel belts. Some dry afternoons in late summer the trail looked like a snake freeway, tracks crossing each other, leaving an intelligible serpent legend for me to read. I paid the most attention to the tracks that were on top.

Once in the Laguna Mountains, I felt privileged to see the very rare and beautiful San Diego Mountain Kingsnake. He was content to let me pick him up and look him over. I also saw a San Diego Ringnecked snake — also beautiful and "friendly."

I sometimes hiked with a colleague, Lisa. One afternoon, we'd taken a longish hike from the Clairemont Mesa parking lot at Mission Trails over to the pond below Highway 52. It was a nice destination for an early summer evening. There were often deer around the pond and always garter snakes swimming. Hummingbirds liked the comparatively humid air above the pond and competed with dragonflies for airspace.

On this particular afternoon, I was a little nervous. It was already six pm and I hadn't seen the snake *du jour*. We were easily five miles from our cars and the daylight would not last forever. My snake vigilance radar was amped up significantly.

Sure enough, as we headed down a pretty shaded part of the trail, the snake *du jour* was there to our left, halfway out of the bush. He wasn't large, twenty inches, but he was awake and alert, ready to hunt. I yelled back at Lisa who was about 15 feet behind me, "Hang on a sec. There's a snake beside the trail here."

"What kind?"

"A rattlesnake. I'll just move him."

"MOVE him? HOW? Oh my God."

With the end of Ol' Gus, I gently encouraged the snake to go back where he'd come from. The snake was amenable. He didn't like me, the stick or my dog. We were not food.

"Oh, Martha. I just peed my shorts!"

I couldn't hold back my laughter. I said, "It's OK. Those shorts are made of wicking material. They'll be dry soon."

Snake-bit

Go forth, under the open sky, and list
To Nature's teachings....

"Thanatopsis" *William Cullen Bryant*.

I've lost three dogs to snakebite. The first, an immense long-legged German shepherd mix, was attracted to the sound of "buzz-worms." The buzz scared most of my dogs, but that guy went AFTER it. Time after time I pulled him away from snakes, but he never learned. One day we were hiking, and he was off leash. He heard a buzz and went for a nest of baby rattlesnakes. He came out with at least 8 full-venomed bites on his hip. I could not possibly afford the antivenin so ended up taking him to the pound to be euthanized. They were kind to me, with compassion for my dog and the situation we were in. I stayed with him until he went over to "the other side."

The other two were bitten in the yard of my home in Descanso, California.

First was Ariel. The saga that led to her death is excruciating, but the end even more so. When I moved into my mountain house, it had been empty for some months. There were hundreds of mice, gophers and ground squirrels. Mice in and outside the house. Snake food everywhere. The weeds were high; no one had cut them for more than a year, and I didn't cut them when I moved in; it was fall and they were on their way out, anyway.

One October afternoon she came in with a red dot on her swollen nose. I wanted it to be a bee sting. My mind did everything it could to make it a bee sting, but it wasn't. On some level, I knew what it was, really, but I didn't want to know. I put her in the truck to go hiking, but looking at her through the back window told me that it was only in my mind that she was going hiking. I took her to my wonderful vet who took one look and said, "It was a snake, Martha. She's been bitten also in her eye."

He told me about the antivenin, but because she'd been bitten in the eye, the poison would go quickly to her brain."I guess we have to put her to sleep," I said, stunned, numb. My vet nodded with his usual gentleness.

"I think it's best," he said.

Ariel and I took so many hikes together in very beautiful places. We watched a mountain lion watch us. We ran through snow drifts and made snow angels together. Ariel was intense, elemental, fierce. A wild animal lived in that somewhat domesticated creature. She was never a pet. She had simply decided in her wolf soul that she loved me. She contained in her ferocity the beauty of the wilderness we loved. Beauty is imperious, elemental, absolute and just; dangerous, the great teacher. Ariel was all of that.

***

When Lupo was a wise, old dog of fourteen he was also bitten by a rattlesnake, perhaps the same one that killed Ariel. His death was sadly sweet. Even Lupo seemed to feel that it was better for him to die that way than to continue the slow degeneration of old age Truffle had. I found him in the backyard with the snakebite on his face. I called my friend Kris because I needed help with Lupo who was a big dog. Kris came down from Julian, a thirty-minute drive.

While I waited for Kris, I sat with Lupo and enjoyed his beauty and his love for me, all our years together. He told me that everything was fine, and I told him it would not be long.

Lupo and Molly at the Medicine Wheel

At the vet, the assistant tried to take my dog from me. "No way you're taking this dog," I said. Lupo was more than my dog. In a way, he was my "man" who cared for me in my years of solitude. When the vet got to the examining room, he shooed the assistant away. Kris and I lifted Lupo onto the table, and I wrapped my arms around my beautiful friend, put his poor snake bitten head on my shoulder. The vet inserted the IV, and within seconds, Lupo was gone.

Kris and I took Lupo's collar up to the Lagunas to put his tag on the post with Ariel's. We hadn't gone far on Sunset Trail when we noticed a coyote walking beside us a few feet to our left. She stayed with us until we were nearly at the post, and I began removing the tag. As I did, I noticed the brand on the collar: Coyote. A shiver went through me. I showed it to Kris. Just as I got the tag off the collar, the coyote crossed the trail about four feet in front of us. She paused to look at us then ran off across the hills, her tail erect like any joyful dog. I looked at Kris, he at me, and we both said, "She took Lupo with her!"

That was Lupo's funeral. He runs forever across those golden hillsides where he rambled so often with me.

Coyotes

"Whenever the pressure of our complex city life thins my blood and numbs my brain, I seek relief in the trail; and when I hear the coyote wailing to the yellow dawn, my cares fall from me - I am happy".
Hamlin Garland

A friend, co-worker, from school was hiking with Molly and me going down a barren rocky slope in the chaparral. My friend, who was behind me, hissed softly, and I turned to see him point to his left. My eyes turned and Molly turned her head in the direction my friend had pointed.

It was the first of many times I shared a hill with a coyote. It also happened that day when I looked at the ground where I had stopped, I found a fossil.

***

I understand that coyotes can be dangerous. They are known to attack, kill and eat domestic dogs and cats. My friend Melanie nearly lost one of her dogs to a coyote, Shelby, one of two rat terriers who were also Lupo's best friends and hiking pals. Shelby was fine after her ordeal, but Melanie was traumatized. Though coyotes rarely attack people, people heighten the danger that does exist by feeding them, enticing them to come close, or leaving trash on the borderlands between their and the coyote world.

Gangs, I mean packs, of Southern California urban coyotes live with people. They use the canyons as freeways and travel through towns without most people even knowing.

In *Wild Thoughts from Wild Places* Dave Quammen writes about the coyotes of LA, not the "coyotes" who were known for smuggling immigrants from Mexico, but the real coyotes, *canis latrans* who were there before the people. The coyotes didn't leave; they adapted.

> What sort of coyote has Los Angeles created? It's a creature that will jump over chainlink for a bowl of Alpo. It's an animal that can learn and remember which storm-sewer channels lead to which golf courses, which duck ponds and swimming pools offer potable water when the hills are dry, which dumpsters behind which supermarkets are likely to overflow with old vegetable and delightfully rancid fish. It's a beast constantly on the alert for unattended barbecued chicken…it's at home on Mulholland Drive. It has eaten from the Tree of Forbidden Knowledge and it recalls fondly the taste of Fifi and Mr. Boots.
>
> I find this neither sad nor inappropriate. Better for the people of Los Angeles to share their city with one slightly corrupted species of Carnivora, I think, than with none at all and the coyote is ideal for the role. It's arguably more similar to *Home Sapiens* in ecological terms if not anatomical ones, than any other species of animal…" (Dave Quammen, *Wild Thoughts from Wild Places*)

When I saw coyotes, I was wandering in their world not they in mine. My interactions with them were positive, often mysterious, frequently goofy.

Native Americans consider coyote to be a trickster because it's difficult to know what a coyote is going to do. Coyotes do seem to be whimsical and curious, and in my encounters with them, I began to see them as extremely intelligent, and, often, silly wild dogs.

One afternoon I had a long conversation with a coyote who sat on a hillside beside my trail. I have no idea what she understood, but I was saying, "Is this cool or what?" and "Wow!" and "I'm talking to a coyote!" and "I wonder what I'm saying?" She responded consistently. Exactly at the moment I'd run out of small talk, and my dogs were getting antsy, she got up, turned away and went over the top of the hill.

I followed the tracks of coyotes on innumerable trails, evaluated the progress of the ripening prickly pear fruit from looking at coyote scat, and listened intently as packs of them yipped and howled outside my window when I lived in Descanso, sometimes inspiring The Models to howl in response. The first month after my return to Colorado, when I lived in a cabin in South Fork, I heard them often and walking my dogs in the darkness, I knew they were all around us.

***

Going often into a landscape, hiking favorite routes daily at nearly the same time, does more than make the landscape familiar. The landscape becomes a kind of home and the hiker a member of a largely invisible family. Without being aware of it, and without planning it, I became a well-known part of the worlds in which I hiked. Wildlife biologists know the best times to see certain animals in certain places in certain seasons. In my experiences with coyotes, I began to wonder if they had figured me out in a similar way:

> *"That human female will probably go up to the Indian Kitchen on this high trail today, don't you think so, Ish-ah?"*
> *"Why are you calling me by my Kumeyaay name?"*
> *"I don't know. Just felt like it. What do you want me to call you?"*
> *"Dude."*

***

One afternoon, with Ariel and Mila — my Chow-chow/Golden retriever mix — on the trail on the trail south Lake Laguna, I turned to ask my dogs (leashed) if they wanted a drink and I found that three coyotes — two adults and a pup — had joined our hike. I had no idea how long they'd been along with us. When I stopped, my dogs sat, as they'd been trained to do, but the coyotes looked at me as if they were saying, "Why are we stopping?"

They stayed with us for another half mile or so and then, for reasons only they knew, they took off across the valley. Maybe their pals were waiting in the trees.

I wondered if there had been other hikes, hikes when I hadn't turned around, and the coyotes had come along. Maybe there were times when my dogs had run free up there, met coyote pals and had adventures.

I will never know.

Apparent Reality

"For too long man has burdened other animals with the aspirations and idealizations of his own society. Only by discarding all myths can he hope to understand himself."

George Schaller, <u>Stones of Silence</u>

Truffle, Molly, Kelly and I hiked up the fire road to North Fortuna Mountain. It had been a wet winter and spring and the stream through Oak Canyon was filled with water. The wild lilac had lost their tiny purple blossoms in the heavy spring rains. In dry years, the petals littered the red path purple; this year they had been pushed into the mud by raindrops.

The fire road leading to the yoke between North and South Fortuna Mountain was steep, but I liked running up hills, and, sorry to say, my limited good sense didn't prevent me from running down, too. If I fell I fell, right? But my knees had both been injured in glamorless stupidity, and I should not — probably — even have been on hills.

Oh well.

***

North Fortuna Mountain is the second highest hill in Mission Trails Regional Park. With much less traffic than Cowles Mountain, I could expect solitude on its steep narrow paths and was seldom obliged to share the top with small talk.

Sometimes, though, the small talk was entertaining like the time some kids at the top, sitting beside full day packs, asked my friend Melanie and me if we had any water. It was a hot day, and we had our dogs, so of course we had a lot of water. We handed them a couple of bottles then asked them what was in their packs.

"Rocks," said one of them.

"Rocks????" I asked. We were ON rocks and surrounded by rocks. "Why?"

"Training for Mt. Whitney."

"Why didn't you put water in your packs?" Melanie asked in wonderment.

"We'd drink it and the packs wouldn't be heavy enough."

"You know," I said, "you could pick up rocks as you drank your water. There are a few around here."

"Whoa, Dude," said one of the kids to the other. I could almost see a lightbulb flash on.

Physical strength alone is not enough. A good hiker needs to think. Dehydration is a real danger.

But usually the top of the mountain small talk was not that entertaining. It was usually stuff like, "That's a hill!"

"Have you climbed Cowles? We usually climb Cowles." (This was bragging. At 1,594 Cowles was higher than North Fortuna by 300 feet.)

"How is this fun?"

"What a view!"

I could agree with the first and last statements; it was a hill and the view was grand. As for Cowles Mountain, I could brag, too, having climbed it four times in one day, but with its crowds, it was not my favorite. As for fun, I didn't know anything more fun than hiking up a hill.

***

My three dogs and I headed back down the hill on the fire road that cloudy afternoon. I tried not to submit to the desire to run (and failed). We ran hooting and whooping and waa-hooing only to be stopped in our tracks by three soaking wet coyotes standing about 15 feet away. They'd — at the very least — run through the stream in Oak Canyon. I held my dogs as the coyotes looked at us. The largest signaled with his head to the others, seeming to say, "Let's not go that way. We'll have to deal with small talk." They turned around, and went north, toward the grove of oak trees for which the canyon had been named.

The rest of the way down the hill we saw the wet evidence of coyote joy in splashes along the dusty trail and paw-prints on the rocks. Once we reached Oak Canyon, my dogs got in the stream themselves. As they played (Truffle fishing, Kelly wading and Molly looking on as she ONLY liked ocean swimming) a solitary woman hiker came up the canyon. She looked at my dogs and then at the muddy footprints on the trail behind her where we had not yet been.

"So YOU'RE the ones who made this big mess!" she said. "I wondered!"

It was a reasonable guess.

Night is Sound

May your trails be dim, lonesome, stony, narrow, winding and only slightly uphill. ...May God's dog serenade your campfire, may the rattlesnake and the screech owl amuse your reverie, may the Great Sun dazzle your eyes by day and the Great Bear watch over you by night.
Edward Abbey, <u>Desert Solitaire</u>

In San Diego, from Thanksgiving to Valentine's Day, while the rattlesnakes hibernated, I often hiked at night. The dogs and I would set out in the late afternoon, enjoy the light of the fading day from a hilltop where I could watch the sun set on the ocean, then turn back to enjoy the purple gray of dusk, the coming of night.

My favorite hike for this experience went under the bridge of the 52 and then outside Mission Trails Regional Park into Spring Canyon. This was also the place I liked best to ride my mountain bike. This trail was good for a night hike because it was not booby-trapped with up-cropping rocks and rain ruts. This was also one place in that urban wasteland where, if the ocean haze did not reach up the San Diego River channel, I could see stars.

Most afternoons, in the company of Ariel and Molly, I'd hike through the light-infused grasslands where, in spring, the ground was covered with wildflowers, through a wash bordered in golden-leafed sycamore and willow, evergreen Coastal Live Oak, to the top of a hill I named the "Goethe-berg," and then back down in the dark.

Night hiking, even in with a full moon, is as different from day hiking as, uh, night from day, largely because it's, uh, dark and it's hard to see. No, I did not use a flashlight. I didn't even own one.

Night hiking requires different alertness, something other than "Watch where you're going." I liked that.

In the oak trees in the bottom of the wash were often at least one — and often two — Western Screech Owls. Most nights I was delighted by their screeching as I approached and passed their tree, but one night they were silent. I sensed they were there. I suspected coyotes. They seemed the most likely reason for the silence of the owls and the sudden alertness of my dogs.

OK, hiking at night is asking for trouble. Large predators are also hiking at night, especially dusk to dark. I knew this, but what's a night hiker to do? I knew I would be wandering around the same trails as cougars and coyotes. I relied on my dogs — which were leashed — to do two things for me, one of which was to sound an alarm. The other was, simply, to smell like dogs.

I yipped. It came pretty naturally. I'd had several conversations with coyotes by then and felt pretty good with the language.

A coyote replied from very nearby, in the wash beside the trail, directly under the owl's tree, a few feet from me. I guessed the owls had dropped a kill and the coyote was taking advantage of an easy meal. It was a plausible story, anyway.

The coyote and I conversed. My dogs laid down.

We carried on our conversation until Ariel got restless. I guess the coyote and I weren't saying anything interesting. More likely, Ariel was hungry.

I gave the coyote one final "Yip" goodbye, and the dogs and I were on our way. The next night it was business as usual for the screeching owls.

Punchin' Cow

I'm an old cowhand from the Rio Grande
But my legs ain't bowed and my cheeks ain't tan
I'm a cowboy who never saw a cow
Never roped a steer cause I don't know how
Sure ain't a fixin' to start in now
Yippie yi yo kayah
                    Johnnie Mercer

    2004, on Labor Day, the end of August, long weekend, a hot Monday afternoon, I hiked the Sunset Trail from the Meadow's Information Station to Laguna Lake. I was with Ariel. We went over the ridge and down the hill leading to the break off from the Sunset Trail to the Big Laguna trail. At the bottom of the hill was an enclosure, recently repaired. The Cedar Fire of October 2003 had burned it. It enclosed a particular kind of flower that a certain butterfly needs. Signs hanging on the wires said, "Butterfly Enclosure". Perhaps it was the streaming endorphins from the long hike, but I found the enclosure hilarious.

Barbed wire or not, there was no way butterflies would stay in a fence like that.

On this day, though, a yearling steer was living a nightmare. The volunteer crew that had repaired and rebuilt that enclosure, had, without noticing, trapped the calf inside.

From the looks and sound of him, he'd been there a couple of days. He was dehydrated and scared; his voice was hoarse from calling to his mother who answered from across the valley. Semi-feral cows, they stayed away from people most of the time. She remained a bit apart, keeping him in view.

His sad little cries really got to me. I walked around the enclosure a couple of times trying to find an opening, but the volunteer crew had done a good job. I tied my dog to a post, filled her dish with water and walked around so I would be near the calf. He was very thirsty. He came right to the fence and drank the bowl dry. I stayed for a while, and watched him strain to defecate. I had seen the trail of terror-diarrhea already on the ground..

When I got home, called the sheriff and left a message. Then I tried a number I thought was the park ranger and left a message. I had plans for dinner so headed into town. When I got back home, there were two messages from a guy named Duncan asking if I could take him to the calf in the morning. I thought he was the Ranger. I had to teach the next morning, so I called him back and tried to explain how to find the calf. He said it would be best if I took him up and showed him. I should have been suspicious.

I was in for it.

***

Duncan picked me up the next morning (missed my first class – YOU choose between teaching English and having an adventure in the mountains with a stranger and a trapped calf) in a beat up silver 1980s Datsun pickup. He was about 65, maybe older, hard to say; his face, his truck, its seats, his hair, his hands were a weathered, textured, grayish version of whatever original color they had been. He wore hearing aids. On the seat beside me, besides pages and pages of old newspaper ads, was *The Confession of St. Thomas Aquinas.*

Duncan was no park ranger. I had no idea who he was, but he thought I should know who he was. In fact, he had done more than any single person to make sure that the little paradise of Descanso Valley remained a paradise of a valley; he also worked very hard to make sure Black Water (mercenary private army) did not build a training facility in our mountains.

Duncan drove like a madman up the Sunrise Highway. Above the noise of the engine, the rattling of the truck bed, and the hum in his ears he made conversation. He asked me where to stop, but when I told him; he argued with me. I got irked. I hiked those trails almost daily, and I knew where the calf was. Finally I said, "I'm the one who told you about the calf; I guess I know where he is."

We stopped and parked where I said and he started walking. Duncan was a rare individual who walked faster than I (I was at 4 mph at the time). When we reached the calf, Duncan said, "That's no calf. That's a *bull*." Indeed, the steer — which I'd described on the phone as "the little guy" — was a lot bigger than I'd remembered.

Duncan had brought bolt cutters and after examining the fence, decided to cut it open in a 24-inch section then we would "steer" the yearling out and into freedom. Duncan would chase the steer, and I would stand with my arms out to the side sort of directing the steer to the opening. Duncan took off his straw hat, got behind the steer and chased him toward me. The calf stopped when he saw me, turned, looked at me with great intensity, and began to paw the ground, his head down. I knew what that was and found it very unfair. We'd had a productive, sharing relationship just the day before when he drank my dog's water. He should have known that I was there to help him. I looked him in the eye, stood completely still, opened my mouth, and screamed. He stopped, distracted by the noise, turned around, jumped over a small fence inside the enclosure, and that was about all Duncan and I could do.

"We need a horse if we're going to do any good here," said Duncan, scratching his head.

"I have to go to work," I said.

Duncan had decided things were funny at that point, but his taciturn personality had alienated me. Sure, we'd just committed a crime in cutting that fence (a fact that interested me a lot) but it hadn't really bonded us at all. Then, as we were about to head out, Duncan said, "I'll just have to call that rancher."

"What rancher?"

"The one who owns the cattle. He has a cowboy up here who can chase that cow outta' there and mend the fence."

"You KNOW the rancher?"

"Sure."

I shook my head and growled to myself. If he knew the rancher, and his phone number, what in the world were we up here for? We had committed a felony!

We kept walking. Duncan was getting pretty silly. "You walk fast for a woman," he said.

"Thanks," I said.

"And you know your way around!"

"Yes." Of COURSE I knew my way around. Grrrrrr. *You grizzled, patronizing jerk,*" I thought.

"Wait, get back," he said suddenly. "Get behind me."

"What?" I froze. Rattlesnake, my first thought. "Snake?"

"No. Cops. Act nonchalant."

We were near the road. The truck was up a hill and behind some trees. I could not see it from where we are standing, but Duncan could. I walked carefully behind him the remaining 100 yards, soon seeing that there was nothing up there but a beat up silver Datsun pickup and a giggling old guy with a cell phone.

Earth's Spine

When we are stricken and cannot bear our lives any longer, then a tree has something to say to us...

Hermann Hesse, <u>Baume</u>

    The two main types of trees in the Laguna Mountains are oak and pine. I came to know the oak trees most intimately through my wood-stove where I burned something we all called White Oak, the hardest, hottest and longest burning, and California Black Oak which was a beautiful red inside. The long drought in Southern California had made life good for the bark beetle. They had been fruitful and multiplied all through the oak forests, a process I witnessed close hand as even the big oaks in my own yard gave up and died. The proscription against moving diseased wood out of the ecosystem meant this beetle-killed wood was often what we burned.

    The other tree was the Jeffrey Pine, a beautiful being who can grow to be hundreds of feet and can live for several centuries. Similar — and related — to the Ponderosa Pine, its needles are the dull green that predominates in those mountains. There are many Jeffrey Pines, all ages, along the trails I hiked.

One that always captured my imagination had died long before I moved to California. When I first saw it in the mid-eighties, I was amazed by its height and its twisted, golden trunk. I took photos looking up through branches that scratched the bright sky.

In the passage of time, the trunk faded from golden to gray. The twisting lines widened as the trunk dried. For more than twenty years I hiked and ran past it. It was my favorite place to stop with Molly, Truffle, Lupo, Kelly, Ariel, Mila and, later, The Models, for a lunch break, or a granola bar and a dish of water.

Then, one snowy day when I was hiking with Jasmine, I reached the tree to find it had fallen across the trail. Broken branches held it above the ground, and though I wanted to climb up on its trunk, it was too high, almost four feet. I sat down on a rock beside it and pondered its long life — at least four or five hundred years.

What had it seen? It had been there for half of my small life, yes, but what else?

The band of snow along the top of the trunk was evaporating, and steam rose from the twists into which the melt water had sunk. I gave Jasmine a drink and shared my granola bar. I asked her what she wanted to do next, but all she did was smile. I decided she wanted to head back. At nine years old, Jasmine was a chubby angelic husky with energy that was soothing, generous and sweet. She also had, and I didn't know it then, cancer in her lymph nodes. I would find it the next year when her neck swelled in what I thought was an abscess. Jasmine's would be the third tag I would suspend from the fence wires on the falling cedar post on the Sunset Trail with Ariel's and Lupo's.

***

Years later, on a quiet, wintry afternoon, hiking with Lily along the south edge of Lake Laguna, I noticed a dozen fallen Jeffrey Pines lying on the broad hillside. Some had fallen in the last hard wind, and some had fallen decades earlier. Over time the branches that had cushioned their fall had decayed, slowly bringing the trunk all the way to the ground. The effect of these long-fallen trees on the tired winter grass was that of a human spine, vertebrae and all, ribs outstretched.

All that remained of the oldest trees was the strongest wood, that from which branches had stretched, a string of individual vertebrae with shreds of ribs clinging tightly to the earth.

"You are earth's spine," I thought to the generations of fallen giants. The fallen trees embraced the Earth, holding it fast.

Home Again

"East wind knows I wish to go to the mountains,
It blows and stops the sound of ceaseless rain between the eaves.
Light clouds on the range wear a cotton-wool cap;
On the treetops the new sun hangs a copper gong"…Su Shih

    After thirty-one years in Southern California, I have returned to live in Colorado, my home state. I live in the San Luis Valley, an Alpine valley as large as Connecticut. It is ringed by mountains, snow-capped, blue and white under a mostly azure sky. The valley floor is varied.

    There are the Great Sand Dunes, rabbitbrush flats, potato and barley fields, the Rio Grande, elk, deer, cougar, coyote, and Sandhill Cranes. There are plains, good for cattle and sheep, fields of grass now golden brown.

    In winter, the bare trees, cottonwood, willow, aspen, send their brittle little fingers into the light. Obvious though it is, it only recently occurred to me that with the leaves gone, more light lands on the ground during the winter. I know, right? Duh…

Sometimes a freezing fog lingers in the Valley and the branches of the trees are covered with hoar-frost, miraculous and crystalline when hit with early morning light.

Mindy on the Monte Vista Golf Course

One winter afternoon not long ago, I stood with Dusty — a Lab/Dobie mix; Mindy — an elderly and arthritic Aussie — and Bear, a young Akbash dog — in the pasture that serves my little town as a driving range in the summer. I looked all around at the mountains and, out of no where, my eyes teared up thinking of one moment, one hike, in San Diego maybe thirty years ago reaching to top of the hump of a hill I jokingly called "Big Dog Health and Fitness Spa." I felt suddenly as if, that day, I had not only been looking at the distant snow-covered Cuyamaca Peak, but years ahead, toward my future, toward this moment in this valley between two mountain ranges, with a river running through it.

I was remembering a day when it had snowed in the Cuyamaca and Laguna Mountains thirty miles to the East, and I had raced up the trail so I could sit against some particular rocks, see the snow on the distant peaks and think of Colorado. I missed snow, I missed skiing, and just being able to see snowy mountains meant so much to me. I thought of the young woman I was back then — thirty years ago, nearly! — and how I had YEARNED.

Beside me that day were my hiking pals, Truffle and Molly. I sat on the moss covered damp red ground, LONGING for the Rocky Mountains. I looked at distant snow covered Cuyamaca Peak until I knew that if I didn't get down soon, it would be dark. It might have been Southern California, but winter evenings carried a bone-chilling, ocean-mist fueled bite, and I hadn't brought a jacket.

As I ran down the hill, the sun dropped lower and tinged Cuyamaca Peak with pale pink Alpenglow. It was dusk when we reached the car. Molly and Truffle jumped up into the back seat, and we went home, past shopping centers and mini-malls and sports bars. I had been eons away from the neon for an hour and glad of it.

I'd climbed that very hill the day before and I would climb it the next day. And the next. And the next. Every day for a year. It was three-quarters of a mile, pretty much straight up, and, thanks to that hill, a year later, I found myself in good enough shape to go farther, go higher.

But more important than that, I'd begun to learn something about what it means to see.

***

What I think of (jokingly) as "my Mt. Everest" was mostly climbed in San Diego at the end of my workdays and on weekends. It was made up mostly of three little "mountains" that my Colorado self, with Rocky Mountain arrogance, had called "hills." I was used to the kind of splendor that can blind you to detail.

Now, back in Colorado, I'm better at being here than I would have been without those hundreds of thousands of feet up and down hills on which most people saw "nothing."

It was absolutely not "nothing."

Mission Trails Regional Park

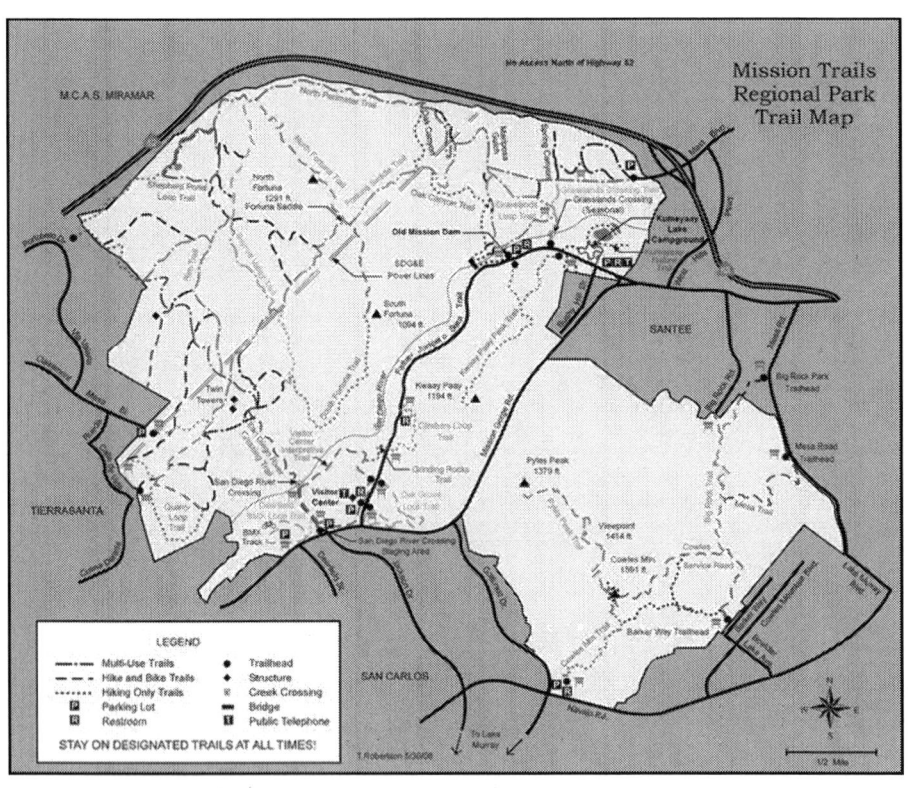

Laguna Mountain Recreation Area

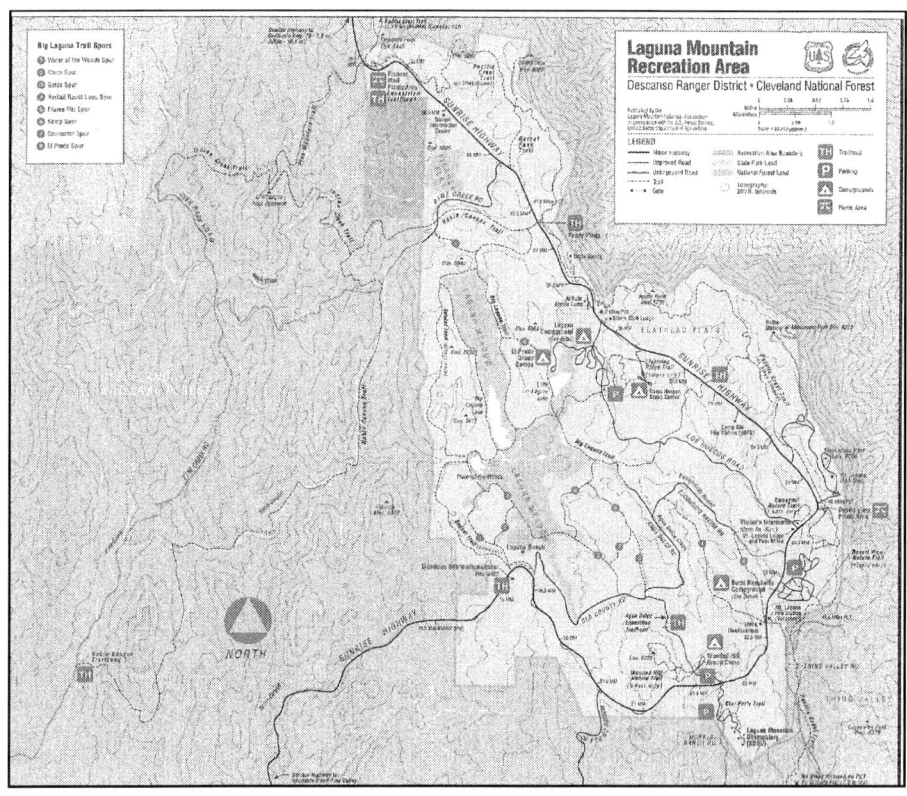

Made in the USA
Columbia, SC
06 June 2018